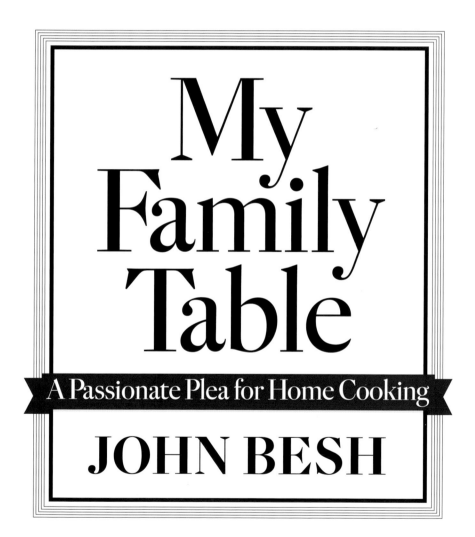

My Family Table

A Passionate Plea for Home Cooking

JOHN BESH

**Andrews McMeel
Publishing, LLC**

Kansas City · Sydney · London

AT OUR FAMILY TABLE:
From left, my boys Andrew and Brendan, my dad Ted Besh, my wife Jenifer, the cook and carver, Jack, my mother Imelda, and Luke.

My Family Table

A Passionate Plea for Home Cooking

JOHN BESH

Andrews McMeel Publishing, LLC
an Andrews McMeel Universal company
1130 Walnut Street, Kansas City, Missouri 64106

www.andrewsmcmeel.com
www.chefjohnbesh.com

11 12 13 14 15 SDB 10 9 8 7 6 5 4 3 2 1

ISBN: 978-1-4494-0787-2

Library of Congress Control Number: 2011923008

Produced and edited by Dorothy Kalins,
Dorothy Kalins Ink, LLC

Book design by Don Morris, Don Morris Design

Photographs by Maura McEvoy

Design editor: Carol Helms

DEDICATION

Of course this book is for my family.
And for your family, too.

It is also for the thousands of parents and children,
brothers and sisters, separated from their
families in defense of our nation, dining on
Meals Ready to Eat so far from those they love,
and so far from their own family tables.

contents

A Passionate Plea for Home Cooking

THIS MAY SEEM A STRANGE CASE for a chef to make, especially one who owns seven restaurants and lives to cook in every one of them; a guy who's clocked many hours cooking on television, running charity fundraisers, etc. And I do not mean to suggest, of course, that we should stop supporting our wonderful local chefs. Far from it.

But today a terrifying wasteland of food options lurks between our kitchen stoves and our favorite restaurants. The packaged foods we use are loaded with salt and sugar and a whole lot of other things that are anything but good for us, our meat is shot up with hormones and antibiotics, our produce is sprayed with God-knows-what, and fast food options are the devil's work. This is not healthy. This is not real. I did not grow up in this kind of world and I don't want my children to grow up this way either.

Whether we work in a kitchen or an office, we all yearn for a different kind of family food experience. Yet I'm only too well aware of the struggles and trade-offs.

I worry that the more cooking becomes entertainment and a spectator sport (instead of a family activity) and the more we fetishize celebrity chefs, the awful result is that we discourage folks from even setting foot in their kitchens. More and more, I'm concerned that by glamorizing chefdom, we turn off the very thing we seek to promote: getting people excited about cooking dinner.

Living through my own television production dramas and being away from my family, I began to realize that what I must do going forward is to put aside such things as food competitions and focus instead on spreading the message of cooking and eating with family and friends. That's why I am writing this book.

Not long after Hurricane Katrina devastated New Orleans, we noticed that our city had an astronomically high rate of children suffering from post traumatic stress disorder. I worked with a local hospital here on a project that brought those very children together to cook. It was a simple idea, to use a communal pot as the catalyst of healing. As I helped these kids chop and brown and stir, I watched barriers fall and the healing begin. Just about all those kids who attended our sessions found true reconciliation by cooking and eating together. It occurred to me that if I can help make a difference—by cooking simply and sharing what I love to cook—I can possibly help us all use our passions and skills to make our lives better at almost every meal.

Our food world today is a cacophony of mass-produced this and instant that, of genetically modified vegetables and prepared, processed, point-and-click meals. Imagine a simple carrot's tortuous journey from the ground to our plate and you'll understand why I'm writing this book. I urge you to set aside manufactured convenience and to cook real food instead. You'll be amazed at what this elemental act does—not only for the people you feed, but for you as well.

My New Orleans, my first book, is a worthy tribute to my home town; in that book I did my best to ensure that tradition and culture is passed on to future generations. But I know every family needs another, more expedient way to cook. Hence *My Family Table*.

chapter one

Kitchen Focus

MASTER RECIPES

"When I apply the same professional logic to my home kitchen…

(the organization of thought that allows me to run seven restaurants) the truth is that cooking and entertaining become pretty much effortless. Organization enables me to cook the kind of lavish meals for our guests that satisfy the senses as well as the soul. I love to dazzle folks with food I create with love. Yes, it sounds a little hokey, but here's the truth: this is why I cook. I consider my role as a chef sort of a noble calling. And what truly allows me to cook for and entertain our guests properly is

Paw's
ONEY
l   Raw

Fresh Organic
Juices

carrot, orange, beet
lemonade, and more!

AMANDA'S FRESH JUICE & POPSICLES

ORGANIC JUICES 8oz for $5

CARROT
BEET-CARROT-APPLE
(16 oz available for $10)

LEMONADES lg$4 sm$2

BEET-LEMONADE
HONEY-LEMONADE

CITRUS & MIXES PRICED AS MARKED

ORANGE SATSUMA $4.50/2.50
PURE ORANGE $4.50/$2.50
STRAWBERRY-ORANGE-PINEAPPLE $5/$2.50

POPSICLES

STRAWBERRY
PINEAPPLE
AVOCADO CREAM $2.50
TAMARIND

KIWI-LIME
CHOCOLATE $2
BANANA
COCONUT

MARKET DAY: Every Saturday the Crescent City Farmers Market comes alive in downtown New Orleans, set against walls painted with murals by Robert Dafford.

two things: having the best ingredients on hand and planning ahead. Don't get me wrong. I'm not saying that I'm ultra-organized. Nor do I claim a lifetime of kitchen focus. Quite the opposite, in fact. My rigor has ripened over the years as I've evolved from cook to chef.

Many years ago, cooking for the Conzen family at their German country house near the picturesque old Roman city of Trier, I decided to cook a meal of locally foraged steinpilz, porcini mushrooms. Well, cook I did— all day and all night—creating what I believed to be a wonderful dinner and, in the process, making a chaotic mess in their kitchen. Though they enjoyed my dinner, Barbara Conzen made a comment that stuck with me forever: she told me the meal was nice, but so very complicated compared to Mario's meals in the same kitchen. Mario, it turned out, was an Italian friend who enjoyed cooking, but seemed to possess a kind of kitchen logic that allowed him to cook effortlessly, bringing out the pure flavors of quality ingredients. This was totally opposite to my approach at the time. So many of us chefs spend way too much of our time over-manipulating foods, attempting to turn them into things they inherently are not. I had a tendency to touch food too much; to combine too many ingredients. I've come to call this style of cooking Confusion Cuisine!

As I've matured, my cooking has become both simpler and more refined. I love to create a dish from just a handful of delicious ingredients. The way I cook at home embodies that approach and this is what I mean by Kitchen Focus. I'm in love with flavor and don't believe it must be sacri-

SHOPPING SMART: Good cooking begins with the best ingredients, like the greens and root vegetables Timmy Perilloux sells right from his truck at the Crescent City Farmers Market, above left. My favorite cane syrup, far left. Citrus from nearby Plaquemines Parish, left, against more of Robert Dafford's "Coffee Man" mural. Resources, page 254.

ficed to simplicity. I joyfully frequent our local farmers' markets and visit my favorite specialty shops because I believe it is urgent that these bastions of quality flourish. I've learned that by keeping my pantry stocked with excellent ingredients, I'll have near-instant meals at my fingertips, meals that taste as if I've toiled over a hot stove all day.

Keeping it simple and delicious means deliberate strategies for planning ahead. I make intensely flavored broths, then freeze them in ice cube trays and empty the cubes into Ziploc bags to keep in the freezer. This obvious trick means I have great restaurant-quality flavor at my finger-tips. Although I spend most of my Sundays cooking the foods of my childhood—the foods I celebrate in my first book, *My New Orleans*—I don't always have that time to devote to wonderful Creole cooking at home. Those recipes demand a level of complexity and a commitment to slow cooking that are at odds with the daily life of a busy family of six. So, in *My Family Table*, I offer an inspiring array of dishes that I love in a different way. With arborio rice in the pantry I can whip up an easy, tasty risotto at the drop of a hat. Why order out when I can construct an amazing curry in minutes with just a few of my essential ingredients?

Too often simplicity means dumbing down recipes; instead I prefer to smarten up strategies. I've built on lessons I've learned the hard way, hoping you won't make the same mistakes I did. My goal is to help you operate with more Kitchen Focus. I urge you to think differently about preparing meals, but think about them you must.

TREATS: I love Richard Sutton's St. James Cheese Company on Prytania Street, top. Fresh turnips and their greens, above. And my current best friend, smoked paprika— pimentón—left.

The Essential Pantry

I'LL BE STRAIGHT WITH YOU. My first book, *My New Orleans*, was based on my personal way with our local ingredients, traditions, and classic dishes. It featured my basic recipes for homemade stocks and wonderful sauces. Authenticity above all was appropriate for that book.

But for *My Family Table*, I want you to make the food, not to worry too much about ingredients or complicated techniques. Sure, I'd rather you put up your own chicken stock from the carcass of last night's roast chicken, but I don't want you to not to make the soup (or braise or stew) just because you only have packaged chicken broth in the house. I think it is so important to keep sight of our goal: to put good, fresh, healthy food on the table for our families. Period.

The first step is to rethink your home pantry with the goal of being so strategically stocked that you're ready for almost anything. Now by pantry I don't mean those sticky bottles and rusting tins and half-filled jars—Lord knows how old—we all have crowding our cupboards. It's time to clear out those shelves and start fresh. Keep in mind that herbs and spices, too, have expiration dates. Everybody has a cheap, generic paprika in their cupboard that tastes of nothing. Upgrade to Pimentón de la Vera, a paprika with a subtle smokiness and a hint of spice—a paprika with flavor! On the following pages you'll find a list of the things I believe we must keep on hand to turn out wonderful meals quickly and beautifully. Buy these ingredients and use them. You'll thank me some Thursday night.

Here's a plan for an almost-instant dinner that I've perfected over the years, using what I have on hand to create a memorable meal: Being prepared absolutely requires a bottle or two of Champagne or Prosecco in the fridge, red wine in the closet. It also demands high-quality pasta in the cupboard. Who doesn't love a great pasta dish? If you're pretty sure you can boil water, the main course is a cinch: with the remains of a roast or braise for a meaty ragout, a drizzle of olive oil, fresh herbs (or dried oregano), and Parmesan cheese grated over the top, it's a perfect main course.

Or how about a sauce of good-quality tuna (canned in oil), with white beans? Pepper jelly is a must because in a minute you can heat it with a touch of vinegar for the perfect sweet/sour/spicy sauce for sautéed chicken breasts. Or, you can add just a dash of hoisin sauce to that pan, turning it into the Korean barbecue sauce I love. This is my idea of kitchen logic.

For an ultra-easy appetizer, I keep a few jars of oil-cured black olives to nibble on while I open a jar of roasted Spanish piquillo peppers that are just begging to be heated in some good olive oil with crushed red pepper flakes and thinly sliced garlic. Slip those peppers on toasted baguette slices and I dare you to find a more perfect bite. Unless, of course, you happen to have a little good salami and/or prosciutto to slice. Dessert is a fruit crumble, served with that amazing ice cream you're smart enough to keep in the freezer. We pick enough berries in season to fill Ziploc bags and freeze. Tossed with flour, sugar, butter, and egg, it's an almost-instant baked dessert.

BROWN JASMINE RICE: This is aromatic jasmine rice with its bran intact. It's often planted with red wild rice, so the two rices are harvested together. This brown rice has big bold flavor and great wild rice texture. Good for you, too.

ARBORIO RICE: The most well-known and available of the short-grain Italian rices. Arborio's versatility and creamy texture make it a staple in my pantry. It's the basic rice for risotto, of course, but it makes a great rice pudding, too.

EXTRA-VIRGIN OLIVE OIL: I have good artisanal olive oils in my pantry, each with its distinct character: woody, spicy, fruity. These are oils to savor, not to cook with: pair with fruit juice as a sauce for fish, stir into tomatoes to add a sheen.

ORGANIC GRITS: These are not instant. Though they'll take a bit longer to cook, the flavor and texture are worth it. I like white organic corn, stone-ground: the larger grains of corn mixed with powdery flour make tastier, creamier grits. Resources, page 254.

ARTISANAL PASTA: Handmade pasta is well worth the extra dollar or two. It requires a little less cooking than factory-made dried pasta, and has far more character. With its earthy taste and firm texture, it actually requires less sauce.

ISRAELI COUSCOUS: Think of this as tiny, dried semolina pasta with a larger grain than its Moroccan cousin. This big grain lets the couscous absorb so much more flavor from the broth it's cooked in. I use it as a substitute for rice in my favorite risotto recipe.

HOT HARISSA: I love to use this spicy North African condiment in my tomato sauces and vinaigrettes. I also like to mix 1 part harissa to 4 parts olive oil and use it as a sauce, marinade, or drizzle for roasted meats and vegetables.

CHERRY TOMATO FIVE-MINUTE SAUCE: I make this sauce, then stash it away (both canned and frozen) for big, robust tomato flavor year-round. It might star in a tomato soup one day and be tossed with fresh pasta the next. Recipe, page 26.

PIQUILLO PEPPERS: This is what the Spanish do so well. Wood-roasted sweet peppers that still taste like peppers. Though they're becoming more available in specialty shops, you can order them online. Perfect right out of the jar. Recipe, page 28. Resources, page 254.

CURRY POWDER: This is one of the easiest to use, go-to spice blends in my pantry because it can either be the star of a somewhat traditional curry dish, or lend an exotic accent to a soup, or perfume a vinaigrette to marinate chicken.

PECAN OIL: This is a flavorful nut oil much like walnut or hazelnut; it adds a refined, toasted, deep nutty flavor to salads and dressings. This oil is meant to be used in very small quantities as it is pungent and a little goes a long way.

PEPPER JELLY: This is one of my favorite down-home funky condiments. In this book I use it as a base for vinaigrettes, in a tasty barbecue sauce, and as a wonderful glaze for grilled chicken and pork Resources, page 254.

ESPELETTE PEPPERS: Ground Piment d'Espelette from the French Basque country is a subtle condiment I use when I want spice that will not overwhelm what I'm cooking. So I add it to more delicate things like seafood and poultry.

PIMENTÓN: This smoked paprika comes sweet or spicy. The peppers have been roasted and smoked so that that the ground powder becomes robust and flavorful. I use it in small amounts to finish a dish. Since it's already roasted, it burns easily. Resources, page 254.

DRIED PORCINI MUSHROOMS: They're expensive, but they're so full of flavor that a little goes a very long way. I briefly soak a small handful in hot water or broth, then use them in mushroom risotto or to flavor stews and sauces.

CHICKEN BROTH: I keep it on hand always because it is truly the base of just about every soup, rice dish, and stew I cook. And what better way to use chicken carcasses, the source of this broth's flavor. Recipe, page 26.

CREOLE MUSTARD: I grew up on this sharp, grainy New Orleans mustard. I add it to sauces, dressings, dips, and marinades. My Favorite Potato Salad (page 173) wouldn't be the same without it. Resources, page 254.

ARTISANAL HONEY: So full of the flavor of their locale, my favorite honeys happen to be our citrus honeys. Look for hyper-local honey at your farmers' market. I use honey in marinades, to sweeten a vinaigrette, and as a sugar stand-in in desserts.

HOISIN SAUCE: A spoonful of hoisin adds a deep, fermented soy flavor that is both sweet and salty at the same time, bringing a balance to noodle dishes and broths. This is a sauce that transcends its Asian roots.

COCONUT MILK: My pantry always has a few cans of unsweetened coconut milk to add a creamy finishing touch to my Madras-style curry. Often I'll use it in place of cream. My wife loves it in black beans with coconut rice.

RICE WINE VINEGAR: Don't think of this as an Asian ingredient! Instead, it's one of my favorite vinegars because its low acidity allows it to be used in so many ways: I add it to everything from barbecue sauce to salad dressings.

RICE NOODLES: Super-quick to prepare (a brief soak in boiling water) and so versatile, rice noodles can be pan-fried or act like vermicelli in a brothy soup. Their neutral flavor works with just about any ingredient.

SAMBAL CHILI PASTE: There's nothing subtle about this thick, garlicky peppery purée, so I use it with discretion when I want big, bold, spicy flavor. I like to use it at the table as a condiment rather than cook with it.

RISOTTO OF ALMOST ANYTHING

Serves 8

The basic method of making risotto will never change: you cook the rice slowly and add broth gradually, so the starchy inside of the rice kernel expands as the outside layer dissolves into creaminess. Risotto feeds the soul and can take a whole range of flavors. I like the pumpkin risotto here, but try a shrimp risotto using shellfish broth, adding a pound of peeled shrimp at the last minute and letting them cook no more than 5 minutes. Or how about a green risotto, with a bunch of watercress or a few handfuls of spinach, chopped fine? Or a mushroom risotto with a pound of sliced fresh mushrooms added to the dried porcini mushrooms.

Keep in mind that there's a lot of bad risotto out there, usually because folks overcook it or add too much wine. But if you do have some white wine open, add a splash or two to the rice and onions, just before you ladle in the broth. It gives yet another dimension of flavor.

1. Heat the olive oil in a large saucepan over high heat and sweat the onions until soft. Add the pumpkin and cook, stirring often, until softened, about 8 minutes. Add the rice, stirring with a wooden spoon to make sure each kernel is coated with oil.

2. Add 3 cups of the hot chicken broth, the rosemary, and porcini mushrooms to the rice. Bring slowly to a boil, then reduce to a simmer. As the broth is absorbed, add more broth and stir often.

3. Cook the rice until it is slightly al dente and most of the broth has been absorbed. The rice should be creamy and porridge-like. This should take about 18 minutes. Then finish the risotto by stirring in the butter and Parmesan cheese. Remove from the heat and season with salt and pepper before serving.

2 tablespoons olive oil	A few dried porcini mushrooms, rinsed
1 onion, diced	2 tablespoons butter
2 cups diced peeled fresh pumpkin	¼ cup grated Parmesan cheese
2 cups arborio rice	Salt
6 cups chicken broth, heated	Freshly ground black pepper
Leaves from 1 sprig fresh rosemary	

CREAMY ANY VEGETABLE SOUP

Serves 8

This potato, leek, and broth base is a wonderful building block for an astounding number of flavorful, velvety soups. The recipe for fennel soup follows, but in place of the fennel, try adding a cup of chopped carrots, or corn off the cob, or chopped broccoli, or diced turnips. I could go on! The method is the same: First, you soften the vegetables, then add the broth and just a bit of cream, simmer, and purée. If you omit all the other vegetables, this becomes the perfect potato and leek soup; serve it chilled and you have a great vichyssoise.

¼   cup olive oil

1   whole leek, trimmed and chopped

½   fennel bulb, trimmed and chopped, tops reserved for garnish

2   cloves garlic, minced

1   potato, peeled and roughly chopped

4   cups chicken broth

½   cup cream

Salt

Freshly ground black pepper

1. Heat the oil in a large heavy-bottomed pot over medium-high heat and sweat the leeks and fennel, stirring, for about 2 minutes. Add the garlic and cook 2 minutes more.

2. Add the potatoes, chicken broth, and cream. Bring to a boil, then reduce immediately to a simmer. Cook until the potatoes are soft, about 20 minutes.

3. Transfer the soup to a blender and purée. Season with salt and pepper. Garnish with chopped fennel fronds.

SIMPLE MEAT RAGOUT FOR ANY PASTA

Serves 8

The tomato/meat base of this ragout will work with any shape of pasta. Just use this recipe as a trusty guide. The point is to use whatever meat you have, such as roast pork (or beef or lamb or poultry), and heat it quickly with canned tomatoes to make a succulent sauce. Keep in mind that the meat is already cooked to perfection, so it takes very little time to come together.

- 2 tablespoons olive oil
- ½ onion, thinly sliced
- 3 cloves garlic, minced
- 2 cups roughly chopped Slow-Roasted Pork Shoulder (page 38) or other cooked meat
- 1 handful dried porcini mushrooms, rinsed
- 2 cups canned diced tomatoes
- 1 cup chicken broth
- 1 teaspoon dried oregano
- 1 dash crushed red pepper flakes
  Salt
  Freshly ground black pepper
- 1 pound pasta
  Parmesan cheese for shaving

1. In a medium heavy-bottomed pot, cook the olive oil and onions over high heat to caramelize the onions, stirring often. After about 5 minutes, add the garlic and cook a few minutes more, stirring. Stir in the meat, mushrooms, tomatoes, and broth, then add the oregano and red pepper. Bring to a gentle boil over high heat, then quickly reduce the heat to low and simmer for 10 minutes. Season with salt and pepper.

2. While the ragout is simmering, cook your pasta. Drain and transfer to a serving dish and ladle the ragout over the pasta. Shave some Parmesan cheese over the top.

THE PERFECT FRITTATA

Serves 1

I think of a frittata as my go-to instant meal. After all, we almost always have eggs in the house, and the frittata can go any way your refrigerator dictates: for breakfast, use ½ cup of cooked diced potatoes and a handful of cooked sausage. For lunch, make a corn and crab frittata with ½ cup of corn and a handful of crabmeat. My favorite dinner frittata is based on Spanish chorizo, olives, and good canned tomatoes.

I like to prepare a frittata the same way I do an omelette, but instead of rolling the cooked eggs onto a plate, I serve the frittata open-face, as with the Zucchini and Mozzarella Frittata here. One trick is to flash the pan into the oven for just few minutes to heat the cheese. But the eggs shouldn't be cooked any longer than with an omelette.

3	large eggs	3	slices fresh mozzarella cheese, in pieces
2	teaspoons canola oil		Salt
¼	cup diced onion		Freshly ground black pepper
¼	cup diced zucchini		

1. Preheat the oven to 400°. In a small bowl, vigorously beat the eggs until frothy. Heat the oil in an 8-inch ovenproof nonstick skillet over medium-high heat. Add the onions and zucchini and sauté until softened and slightly golden, about 3 minutes. Add the eggs and use a spatula to swirl them around the pan. Gently lift up the edges of the eggs to evenly disperse the liquid.

2. Once the eggs have begun to firm up, scatter the mozzarella over the top. Put the pan in the oven for 2–3 minutes, or until the eggs are just set. Hold a large plate over the skillet and invert the skillet so the frittata drops onto the plate. Slice into wedges, season with salt and pepper, and serve it up!

MASTER RECIPE

CURRIED ANYTHING

Serves 8

Recipes for curries vary almost more than any other dish, which is great because you can hardly go wrong. Curries make delicious use of last night's roast pork, chicken, beef, or seafood, and they are a wonderful way to serve just vegetables as a main course. Use 2 cups of cooked meat, as in our family staple here, Eggplant and Chicken Curry; it's Brendan's favorite. Or make a curry of cauliflower florets and sugar snap peas as a meatless variation. Either way, make it as spicy as you wish, tasting as you go, adding small amounts of curry powder and chili paste until the heat is just right for you.

Curry powder is a combination of spices whose potency varies with the manufacturer, some have more cumin and coriander, others more ginger and chili powder. Since this isn't a book about the nuances of South Asian cooking, I'll not insist you make your own, but I do hope you'll sample a few curry powders to find your favorite. As for rice, use what you have, but I love basmati and jasmine rice. You can even use brown rice.

1. Melt the butter in a large saucepan over high heat, add the eggplant, and sauté until soft. Add the ginger, green onions, and garlic. Sprinkle the curry powder into the pan and toast for a moment. Add the squash and potatoes, stirring to coat them with the spices.

2. Continue to stir for a few minutes, then add the coconut milk, broth, and chili paste. Bring to a gentle boil, add the chicken, then reduce the heat and simmer for 15 minutes. Season with salt and pepper and serve over rice.

2 tablespoons butter	1 13-ounce can coconut milk
1 eggplant, unpeeled, diced	1½ cups chicken broth
2 tablespoons peeled and minced ginger	¼ teaspoon sambal chili paste
2 green onions, chopped	2 cups chopped cooked chicken
2 cloves garlic, crushed	Salt
2 teaspoons Madras curry powder	Freshly ground black pepper
1 summer squash, diced	4 cups cooked rice
1 potato, peeled and diced	

WARM ANY FRUIT CRUMBLE

Serves 8

The name really does say it all. You can use 3 cups of any fruit or berries for a delicious and almost-instant dessert. From the figs used here, to peaches or raspberries, this crumble works. And see page 240 for Brendan's Apple and Pear Crumble. Crumbles can be assembled well in advance and cooked when you're ready. I like to serve them right out of the oven with a scoop or two of ice cream; it's hard to imagine a more satisfying dessert.

1. Preheat the oven to 400°. Toss the fruit in a mixing bowl with the egg, brown sugar, flour, melted butter, and cinnamon to coat. Spoon the fruit mixture into individual ramekins or into one big baking dish.

2. For the topping, combine the flour, brown sugar, granulated sugar, cinnamon, and salt in a medium bowl. Cut the butter into the mixture until the topping is crumbly. Sprinkle over the fruit.

3. Bake until the fruit is bubbly and the topping turns a lovely golden brown, about 25 minutes. Serve warm with ice cream.

FOR THE FRUIT

- 3 cups figs, stems removed, or any other chopped fruit or berries
- 1 egg, lightly beaten
- 3 tablespoons brown sugar
- 2 tablespoons all-purpose flour
- 2 tablespoons butter, melted
- 1 pinch cinnamon

FOR THE TOPPING

- ⅔ cup all-purpose flour
- ⅓ cup packed brown sugar
- ¼ cup granulated sugar
- ½ teaspoon cinnamon
- 1 pinch salt
- 6 tablespoons butter, cut into ½-inch pieces

STICKY HANDS: Luke is a master cookie maker and loves to get his fingers in the sweet topping of a crumble.

MASTER RECIPE

QUICK PICKLED VEGETABLES

Makes 1 quart

I like to use this process to pickle carrots, radishes, and beets and have come to prefer the texture of these homemade pickles to anything store-bought. The vegetables are blanched for a moment, leaving them still crisp. Although these pickles taste wonderful alone, they are so beautiful I frequently use them as a way to elevate many dishes, especially the Vietnamese-inspired recipes in this book.

½ teaspoon salt

1 pound baby carrots, radishes, or beets, peeled

1 cup sugar

1 cup rice wine vinegar

1 tablespoon Zatarain's Crab Boil seasoning, or 1 teaspoon each of mustard seeds, coriander seeds, and black peppercorns

1. In a medium saucepan, bring 2 cups of water to a boil along with the salt. Add the peeled vegetables and blanch for no longer than 2 minutes. Remove the vegetables with a slotted spoon. Add the sugar, vinegar, and spices to the pot and bring just to a boil.

2. Fill canning jars with the blanched vegetables and pour in enough cooking liquid to fill the jars. Cool, then cover and store the jars in the refrigerator where they'll last for a couple of weeks.

CHICKEN BROTH
Makes 2½ quarts

Of course you can always make a broth from the carcass of a roast chicken, but here's a quicker strategy that yields another meal in the process. The poached chicken is perfect for chicken salad or to use in any of our ragouts over pasta, and the resulting broth can be the base for any soup or risotto or stew in this book.

1 whole chicken (organic if possible)	2 carrots, peeled and roughly chopped
2 onions, peeled and quartered	6 cloves garlic, crushed
2 stalks celery, roughly chopped	2 bay leaves

1. Put all the ingredients into a large heavy-bottomed pot and add water to cover by 3 inches. Place the pot over high heat and bring to a boil. Once boiling, reduce the heat to a low simmer and simmer slowly for an hour.

2. Remove the chicken from the broth and set aside for other uses. Strain the broth and discard the vegetables. Reserve the broth in jars in the refrigerator, or freeze what you don't use immediately. Your pantry will benefit.

SHELLFISH BROTH

1. Substitute 2 pounds of shrimp, crab, or lobster shells (or a combination of all three) for the chicken. Place the shells in a roasting pan and roast in a 400° oven for 15 minutes. Then add them to the stockpot with the other flavoring ingredients.

CHERRY TOMATO FIVE-MINUTE SAUCE
Makes 1½ quarts

This sauce is full of the fresh, vibrant flavor of tomatoes picked straight from the vine. I like the sweetness of cherry tomatoes and I find that when I grow them, they ripen all at once and I have more than I can possibly use. That's the time to think of winter, when you can't find a fresh tomato anywhere. I preserve the sauce in jars, or even easier, I store it in quart containers in the freezer.

¼ cup olive oil	Leaves from 4 sprigs fresh basil
2 quarts ripe cherry tomatoes, halved	Salt
2 teaspoons crushed red pepper flakes	Freshly ground black pepper
4 cloves garlic, crushed	

1. Heat the oil in a large saucepan over high heat. Add the tomatoes, pepper flakes, and garlic and bring to a boil. Reduce the heat to medium and cook for another 5 minutes, stirring occasionally with a wooden spoon. Add the basil.

2. Pour the sauce into a food mill and purée. Season with salt and pepper. Transfer the sauce to Ziploc bags or quart containers and store in the freezer.

COUSCOUS WITH SPICY CHICKEN

Serves 4–6

Couscous belongs in every pantry because of its versatility and ease of use. Too often, couscous is confused with cracked wheat, when in fact it is really the smallest of all pastas. I think it's under-appreciated because it's associated with a long steaming process. But it doesn't have to be that way and I don't think you sacrifice much using quick-cooking couscous. I like to perfume couscous with a touch of turmeric or saffron, spices that I believe should be in every pantry. I often serve this dish with a touch of olive oil and harissa (the spicy Moroccan condiment of crushed chiles, tomato, and spices) for an extra kick.

FOR THE SPICE BLEND AND CHICKEN

- 1 teaspoon ground ginger
- 1 teaspoon fennel seeds
- 1 teaspoon coriander seeds
- ½ teaspoon red pepper flakes
- ½ teaspoon cinnamon
  Salt
  Freshly ground black pepper
- 1 roast chicken, cut into pieces
- 2 tablespoons olive oil

FOR THE COUSCOUS

- 2 tablespoons vegetable oil
- ½ head cabbage, chopped
- 1 carrot, peeled and chopped
- 2 green onions, finely chopped
- 1 clove garlic, sliced
- 2 cups couscous
- 1 teaspoon turmeric
  Salt
- 2 cups chicken broth
- 1 tablespoon butter
  Freshly ground black pepper
  Leaves from 2 sprigs fresh mint, chopped
  Harissa, optional

1. Preheat the oven to 350°. For the spice blend, toast the ginger, fennel, coriander, red pepper, and cinnamon in a small skillet over medium heat for 2 minutes. Stop and smell the aroma! Put the spices in a spice grinder or mortar and pestle and process to a fine powder.

2. Salt and pepper the chicken and toss it with the olive oil and the spice blend in a large bowl. Transfer the chicken to a baking sheet and bake for 15 minutes, or until it's hot. You're just reheating the chicken.

3. For the couscous, in a medium saucepan combine the oil, cabbage, carrots, green onions, and garlic. Cook over medium-high heat, stirring, for 3–5 minutes, until soft. Add the couscous with the turmeric and a pinch of salt. Stir to make sure that all the grains are coated with oil, then add the broth.

4. Bring to a simmer, remove from the heat, and cover. Let stand until the couscous is tender and the water is absorbed, 5–7 minutes. Fluff with a fork to make sure there are no lumps, then add the butter and mix well. Season with salt and pepper and add the mint.

5. Mound the couscous in a bowl and top with the spiced chicken. Serve with harissa and drizzles of olive oil.

PASTA WITH ROAST CHICKEN & TOMATOES
Serves 6

We're used to carbonara with bacon or ham, but here's another take on the idea. I like to use the meat from our beautiful Herb-Roasted Chicken (page 40), but any good cooked chicken will work. Or sauté a few chicken breasts briefly in some olive oil instead. No pine nuts? No problem. Use whatever nuts you have on hand. Keep in mind that you might want to add a bit more chicken broth to your "tomato gravy" if it appears a bit too thick.

¼ cup olive oil	2 cups chopped cooked chicken
1 onion, chopped	½ cup chicken broth
2 cloves garlic, minced	¼ cup chopped piquillo pepper
½ teaspoon Espelette or cayenne pepper	¼ cup olives, pits removed
2 cups chopped fresh tomatoes, or 1 12-ounce can diced tomatoes	1 pound fettuccine or other pasta
¼ cup red wine	2 tablespoons pine nuts, toasted
1 teaspoon sugar	2 tablespoons grated Parmesan cheese
Leaves from 1 sprig fresh rosemary	

1. Heat the olive oil in a large skillet over high heat. Add the onions and cook, stirring, until browned, about 5 minutes. Reduce the heat to medium high and add the garlic and Espelette pepper. Stir for another minute, then add the tomatoes, wine, sugar, and rosemary. Bring to a boil and add the chicken, chicken broth, piquillo peppers, and olives. Reduce the heat to low and simmer, covered, for about 10 minutes.

2. Meanwhile, bring a large pot of salted water to a boil over high heat. Add the fettuccine and cook for 11 minutes. Drain.

3. When the pasta is done, add it to the skillet and toss well in the sauce to coat. Transfer the pasta and chicken to a serving platter and scatter the toasted pine nuts and Parmesan over the top.

I LOVE PIQUILLO PEPPERS
Serves 8

Piquillo peppers are imported from Spain, where they're roasted over wood fires in the northern town of Lodosa, hence their rich, smoky flavor. I fell in love with them years ago in Spain, where I discovered not just how tasty they are, but how easy it is to use them. Piquillos right out of the jar become a simple salad when tossed with a fruity vinaigrette. Or stuff them with goat cheese or Ratatouille (page 48) and bake quickly with a little olive oil and herbs. I often serve piquillos from a small saucepan, as in the recipe below, sautéed with garlic (or mushrooms or both). They're perfect on grilled toasts in this quick appetizer whose aroma takes me back to Spain every time I serve it. Resources, page 254.

¼ cup olive oil	Salt
1 cup roasted piquillo peppers, halved	Freshly ground black pepper
3 cloves garlic, thinly sliced	Slices of baguette, toasted
1 teaspoon crushed red pepper flakes	Leaves from 1 sprig fresh basil, thinly sliced

1. Heat the olive oil over medium-high heat in a small saucepan. Add the peppers, garlic, and red pepper flakes and cook for 5 minutes. Season with salt and pepper. Remove from the heat, serve from the pan with a plate of grilled toasts on the side. Sprinkle the basil on top.

CARBONARA WITH SWEET PEAS & HAM

Serves 6

I always have a bit of good baked ham on hand because our family loves to make carbonara. Even if fresh green peas are not in season, I always keep a few packages of frozen peas in the freezer just so we can make this recipe easily. I've often substituted fava beans, lima beans, or shelled soy beans for the sweet peas, for interesting takes on this classic Italian dish.

1   pound linguine

2   tablespoons olive oil

½   cup diced ham, such as from Pecan-Baked Ham (page 42)

2   cloves garlic, minced

1   cup sweet peas
    Leaves from 1 sprig fresh thyme

½   teaspoon crushed red pepper flakes

1   cup cream

1   egg yolk

¼   cup grated Parmesan cheese

1   dash nutmeg
    Salt
    Freshly ground black pepper

1. Bring a large pot of salted water to a boil over high heat. Add the linguine and cook for 11 minutes. Drain.

2. While the pasta is cooking, heat the olive oil in a skillet over medium-high heat. Add the ham and garlic and sauté gently just until the garlic is softened. Add the peas, thyme, and red pepper and cook until the peas are just heated through. Add the cream and let simmer for a minute.

3. Add the cooked linguine to the skillet and mix to combine. Turn off the heat and mix in the egg yolk. Add the Parmesan cheese and nutmeg and mix well. Season well with salt and pepper and serve it up right from the pan.

JENIFER IN ACTION: As queen of the stove on weekdays, she'll frequently turn out a quick carbonara with Luke's help.

"Sundays begin way too early around here…

especially for a guy like me in the restaurant business. I hit the kitchen at first light, just as the bayou behind our house wakes up to the day, birds chattering in the cypress and tupelo trees that catch and hold the sunrise. First, I'll organize breakfast, and since breakfast is usually a big meal at our house on weekdays, today I'll make something simple, sweet, and small, like beignets or cinnamon buns, before we're dressed and off to Mass. After church, we'll probably stop at the grocery for something or other we forgot. Then home.

SUNDAY TABLE: Olive Oil–Roasted Cauliflower, String Beans with Garlic, and Field Peas, top. Luke peppers the roast, above. Opposite, clockwise from right, Jack and me; our pork roast; little hands at work; essential herbs and twine for tying.

Sunday suppers are my escape. I lose myself in cooking, I hide away from the world among my little boys—their kitchen chatter works magic to transport me far away from the pressures of work. On Sundays, I cook for myself in totally different ways than in my restaurants. It becomes purely a cooking of the heart. I assign each of the boys a kitchen task, and I wish I could describe the joyful feeling of everything being right with the world (if only for a few minutes) as I look over my shoulder and see Brendan slicing an onion (properly!), or Drew Drew peeling garlic, or Jack kneading dough, or Luke carefully measuring ingredients, or Jenifer relaxing for a change, just sipping a glass of wine.

My Sunday supper menu always follows the traditions of our Southern roots, inspired by my Grandmother Grace's Southern classics. I want my children to be able to identify where they come from through the foods they eat. The centerpiece of Sunday supper is invariably a roasted something. Depending upon the weather, side dishes will range from hot and substantial to cool and light. Desserts are nothing fancy, just delicious, usually cakes and pies based on whatever's in season.

You see, in my neck of the woods, Sunday is a time for family and friends, even though it's impossible to distinguish who's family and who's friend. On any given Sunday we could easily have 20 to 40 guests come by, some for a drink, others for supper, still others will take food home. And when friends don't drop by, we'll reach out to them because it always happens that I've cooked lots extra. The tradition of the Sunday feast is a worthy one and accomplishes so much more than just feeding us. It nurtures us, it nourishes our souls. Sunday is the day when we can slow down and distance ourselves from distractions like shopping and video games and television and try to connect with each other. (Except if the New Orleans Saints are playing; on Saints' game days, we'll still eat, though only at halftime.)

I know I am not alone in my craving for quiet family and friend time. I've seen it in our young cooks at the restaurants who'll get together on their day off because their real families may be thousands of miles away. They recognize the importance of cooking and eating together as a community of friends. Given our crazy, busy schedules, we all need to just slow down. To recharge and rejuvenate. What better way to do it than on a Sunday, in the kitchen, and at the table with people you love?

How I Cook a Roast

ROASTING A CHICKEN is perhaps the easiest thing that can be done in a kitchen, and the tastiest dish when done right. Yet I hear over and over again how folks have serious hang-ups about proper roasting. Hence, the pre-cooked bird from the supermarket. Here's the deal: It's short work to season a roast and put it in the oven. In fact, if I'm going to fire up the oven on Sunday, then I'll make the most of it and roast a few things at a time.

To roast is to cook with dry heat, which means you don't cover the meat you're cooking and you certainly don't submerge it in any sort of liquid. Let's take the pork shoulder, better known as the Boston butt. It's best roasted at a low temperature, because it's a big cut of meat (about 5 pounds) and it needs time to cook through. The first thing is to season the meat with lots of salt and pepper. Then I'll cook it one of two ways.

One way is to sear it in a large skillet, dress it up with a few hearty herbs like rosemary, sage, and thyme, and then put it in a roasting pan with a couple of onions, carrots, celery stalks, and garlic cloves. I'll pour a little water into the pan, so that all the drippings from the pork roast don't burn on the bottom, and those delicious drippings can be used for a pan sauce. I put the pan in a low oven, say 250°–325°.

The second way is to not sear the meat first. Instead, I'll season it with salt and pepper and then prick the fatty side of the pork with a paring knife and insert small slices of garlic and some of those hearty herbs. I'll put the roast in a pan, fat side up, on top of a bed of aromatic vegetables (onions, carrots, celery), then into the preheated 450° oven and quickly reduce the heat to 250°. This way, the surface of the meat will begin to brown as if it were seared in a pan, but when I reduce the heat, it'll cook low and slow. I put the roast in fat side up and larded with herbs; as the fat renders it will baste itself with those succulent flavors.

Either way, as long as I have the oven cranking, I'll go ahead and prepare a chicken for the roasting pan, slathering a fine, farm-raised bird with olive oil, sea salt, pepper, and herbes de Provence, and stuff the cavity with garlic. I'll throw that chicken into the oven at the same time as the pork roast, or right after, in a moderately hot oven, say 400°, for about 45 minutes, until it is brown and smells like a warm afternoon in Provence. Either way, I've easily provided another dinner for the family to eat later in the week.

That's why I think of Sunday roasts as money in the bank. See Chapter 4, School Nights, for ideas for easy meals of pasta, soups, salads, and sandwiches to make from Sunday's roast.

BASIC PAN SAUCE FOR ALL ROAST MEATS

2 tablespoons fat from pan drippings	1 cup chicken or beef broth
2 tablespoons flour	1 sprig fresh thyme
½ shallot, minced	Salt
Aromatic vegetables, strained	Freshly ground black pepper

1. In a small saucepan over medium-high heat, heat the fat. Stir in the flour and keep stirring for 3 minutes.

2. Add the shallot and stir for a couple of minutes. Stir in the aromatic vegetables for a minute more. Add the broth, stirring so that no lumps form. Bring to a boil, then reduce the heat to medium low, add the thyme, salt, and pepper, and let the sauce simmer for a few minutes.

SLOW-ROASTED PORK SHOULDER

Serves 10–12

You'll notice I often add a bit of water, about a half inch, to the bottom of my roasting pans to keep the savory meat drippings from burning. These tasty drippings—along with the strained aromatic vegetables that have softened in the fat that bathes the roast—are the makings for the incredible-tasting Pan Sauce, above. Once roasted, this pork turns into Jambalaya (page 70), Ragout of Pasta (page 17), and Easy Pork Grillades (page 94).

1 4–5-pound boneless pork shoulder	3 garlic cloves, thinly sliced
Salt	2 onions, chopped
Freshly ground black pepper	1 carrot, peeled and chopped
4 sprigs fresh rosemary	1 stalk celery, chopped
	Butcher's string

1. Preheat the oven to 325°. Season the shoulder liberally on all sides with salt and pepper. Truss the roast by tying one length of butcher's string around the roast lengthwise and pulling taut. Then tie 4 shorter strings widthwise, each about an inch and a half apart.

2. Place the roast fat side up. With a paring knife, make many small cuts in the fat. Cut the rosemary sprigs into 1-inch pieces and insert a sprig halfway into every other cut. Slip the garlic slices into the remaining incisions.

3. Scatter the chopped onions, carrot, and celery in the bottom of a heavy-bottomed roasting pan. Set the shoulder on top of the vegetables and add about ½ inch of water to the pan. Roast for about 2½ hours, or until

the pork registers an internal temperature of 155° on a meat thermometer. Strain the vegetables and reserve with the pan juices for a future soup, or make a Pan Sauce, opposite.

4. At our house, we slice and serve this pork roast with Olive Oil–Roasted Cauliflower (page 48) and Provençal Stuffed Tomatoes (page 56).

HERB-ROASTED CHICKEN
Serves 4

Herbs play a great role in elevating a roasted chicken, but too many varieties or too much of one kind can create herbal warfare. More is not better! After you carve and serve the chicken, make sure to save the chicken carcass and the drippings. Those bones with all their rich flavor are perfect for stock. And if you're not ready to make stock right away, just wrap the carcass well and freeze it.

Pan drippings are pure gold. Any time you strain the liquid from the vegetables, you'll have equal proportions of fat and natural juice. Refrigerate that for a day, and the fat will solidify and rise to the top. Then remove the chicken fat and save it separately to use for making a roux or sautéing vegetables. The strained juices make a natural sauce for roast chicken, or add them to a soup for a great hit of flavor, or make a delicious Pan Sauce (page 38).

RAINBOW CARROTS: Our farmers now grow white, yellow, red, as well as carrot-colored carrots. Quickly steamed and flecked with herbs, they light up any plate.

1	4-pound whole free-range organic chicken
	Salt
	Freshly ground black pepper
1	head garlic, halved
2	tablespoons olive oil
	Leaves from 1 sprig fresh thyme, chopped
	Leaves from 1 sprig fresh rosemary, chopped
	Leaves from 1 sprig fresh sage, chopped
1	onion, chopped
1	carrot, peeled and chopped
1	stalk celery, chopped
	Butcher's string

1. Preheat the oven to 400°. Season the chicken cavity liberally with salt and pepper and stuff the halved head of garlic inside. Season the outside of the chicken with more salt and pepper, then slather on the olive oil. Scatter the chopped thyme, rosemary, and sage all over the chicken, letting the leaves cling to the oiled skin.

2. To truss the chicken, cut a length of butcher's string 4 times longer than the chicken. Set the chicken on a board, breast side up. Find the middle of the string and slip it beneath the tail. Bring the ends of the string up and across the tail, crossing the string over the ends of each drumstick from the inside. Loop around the drumstick once or twice and pull the string taut. Then turn the chicken over and cross the strings across the back of the chicken, centering one end over each wing. Turn the chicken over and pull the strings tight to secure the wings against the body. Tie the ends in a knot and cut off the excess string.

3. Scatter the onions, carrots, and celery in a heavy-bottomed roasting pan, then pour in enough water to cover the bottom of the pan. Place the chicken, breast side up, over the bed of vegetables. Roast for about 45 minutes, or until the chicken breast registers an internal temperature of 150° on a meat thermometer and the legs register 160°. The skin should be dark amber and when you move the joint at the crease of the thigh, the juices should run clear. Let the chicken rest for 30 minutes before serving.

PECAN-BAKED HAM

Serves 12

Chances are you won't find a really good cooked or smoked ham in the supermarket. It's hard to determine quality by looks alone. All I can say is never use canned ham, and search out a good Italian butcher or ask at your farmers' market for the best local cooked ham.

In the South, we pretty much have pecans coming out of our ears. As a matter of fact, there's nothing our pigs like more than pecans. We like to coat our hams with pralines, those sweet candies made in New Orleans. But brown sugar and butter will work almost as well if you're careful to use soft butter and make sure to mix all the ingredients well before you slather the mixture on the ham.

¼   cup chopped pecans

1   cup brown sugar

1   tablespoon Chinese five-spice powder

2   tablespoons butter, softened

1   5-pound good quality cooked ham

2   medium onions, chopped

1. Preheat the oven to 350°. In a small bowl, mix the pecans, sugar, and five-spice powder with the butter until you have a fine, crumbly mixture. Rub generously over the ham, patting the crust with your hands.

2. Scatter the onions in the bottom of a heavy roasting pan and add about 2 cups water. Place the ham on the bed of onions. Slide the pan into the oven and roast for about 2 hours, checking to make sure there's still liquid in the pan. As the water evaporates, add a bit more. The ham is done when a nice glaze forms on the outside.

3. The pecan mixture and the water in the pan will create their own sauce to pour over the ham after you've sliced it into beautiful pink rounds. If the sauce seems too thin, just pour into a saucepan and reduce it.

PERFECT ROAST LEG OF LAMB

Serves 10–12

Try to find lamb that is pasture-raised and hormone- and antibiotic-free. It makes a great difference (to us and to them). The quality of the meat and being mindful not to overcook it is the secret to lamb perfection. We have a great farmer near Opelousas, Louisiana, who raises an old breed of sheep called Gulf Coast. Meat from his lambs is extra-fatty, which I love. As the leg of lamb roasts, I make sure to take several temperature readings in various parts of the leg to assess doneness.

1 6–7-pound leg of lamb, bone in	Leaves from 2 sprigs fresh marjoram, chopped
Salt	
Freshly ground black pepper	Leaves from 2 sprigs fresh thyme, chopped
2 teaspoons crushed red pepper	1 onion, chopped
	2 carrots, peeled and chopped
2 tablespoons olive oil	
Leaves from 2 sprigs fresh rosemary, chopped	2 garlic cloves, minced
	Zest of 1 lemon

1. Preheat the oven to 450°. Season the lamb generously with salt and black and red peppers, then massage the leg with the olive oil, rosemary, marjoram, and thyme.

2. Scatter the chopped onions, carrots, and garlic in the bottom of a heavy-bottomed roasting pan. Set the lamb on top of the vegetables. Sprinkle lemon zest over the lamb in the pan.

3. Put the pan in the oven and reduce the temperature to 250°. Roast the lamb for 1 hour or so, until the meat registers an internal temperature of 135° on a meat thermometer. Strain the vegetables and reserve the pan juices for Pan Sauce (page 38).

4. Ratatouille (page 48) would be wonderful with the lamb, along with Sweet Corn Pudding (page 54).

CRISPY ROAST DUCKLINGS

Serves 6

It's really important to find big, six-pound ducks to roast and well worth placing a special order with your butcher, because with smaller ducks the breasts have a tendency to turn tough and dry. Not good. You know the duck is perfectly cooked when you're able to grab the drumstick with a kitchen towel and twist it with relative ease.

2 6-pound ducks	1 onion, diced
2 bay leaves	2 large turnips, peeled and chopped
1 head garlic, halved	
Salt	1 bunch baby carrots, peeled
Freshly ground black pepper	6 shallots, halved
1 tablespoon dried thyme	Butcher's string

1. Preheat the oven to 325°. In the cavity of each duck, place a bay leaf and half head of garlic. Tie the legs together with butcher's string. Season the ducks generously on all sides with salt, pepper, and the thyme.

2. Scatter the onions, turnips, carrots, and shallots in a heavy-bottomed roasting pan and pour in enough water to cover. Set the ducks, breast side up, on top of the vegetables. Roast for about 2 hours, or until the ducks' skin turns mahogany.

3. It's incredible to serve the whole ducks on a large platter ready to be carved at the table. I surround them with Rosemary & Garlic Roast Fingerling Potatoes (page 50). As the ducks rest on the platter, their juices mingle with the potatoes.

PORK RIB ROAST
Serves 8

The good news is that better pork (sustainably raised, with true flavor and marbled texture) is increasingly available. But if you can't find good pork, order it from your butcher. We raise our own Mangalitsa, or wooly, pigs for all our restaurants, not just because it's good farming practice, but because I love the meat. I like to leave a fair amount of fat on the roast, so that the lean pork flesh is basted by this glorious fat and flavored with the aromatic herbs.

1 5–6-pound standing pork rib roast, bone in, with chine removed
Salt
Freshly ground black pepper
1 tablespoon herbes de Provence

1 onion, chopped
1 carrot, peeled and chopped
1 stalk celery, chopped
3 garlic cloves, crushed

1. Preheat the oven to 350°. Season the pork generously all over with salt, pepper, and the herbes de Provence.

2. Heat a heavy-bottomed roasting pan over high heat. Add the pork roast and sear on all sides until it turns a lovely golden brown. Remove the pork roast from the pan and turn off the heat.

3. Add the onions, carrots, celery, and garlic to the bottom of the pan and cover with water. Set the pork on top of the vegetables and roast for 1–1½ hours, until the meat reaches an internal temperature of 145°. Let the meat rest for a moment before slicing into individual chops, each with its own bone.

4. These roasted pork chops just cry out for Perfect Mashed Potatoes (page 51) and String Beans with Garlic (page 51).

SLOW-COOKED
BEEF CHUCK ROAST

Serves 12

For eight years we have raised our own Charolais cattle on rolling, grassy pastures north of New Orleans. It's the beef we have at our house. My brother-in-law Patrick and I usually split a steer cut into roasts, chops, and steaks. Of course, a big freezer is the only way to afford and keep good beef. It's important to remember that pasture-raised beef is so lean that you have to cook it differently, which means less cooking time and at lower heat.

I strongly recommend pasture-raised beef and generally roast the beef to about rare, knowing that once I pull it out of the oven it will continue to cook to medium rare. You may even want to remove your roast from the oven a little bit sooner; what matters is not to overcook it. I add the potatoes and garlic at the beginning of the roasting process, so that they will roast to deliciousness in the beef drippings.

HAPPY COWS: I have long believed in the superiority of pasture-raised beef for us, for them, and for the planet. With my old friend, Chris Meredith, right, we raise Charolais cattle. There they are above, grazing on real grass!

1	4–5-pound beef chuck roast
	Salt
	Freshly ground black pepper
4	tablespoons unsalted butter, softened
	Leaves from 2 sprigs fresh thyme
1	onion, chopped
2	carrots, peeled and chopped
2	pounds fingerling potatoes
1	head garlic, cloves separated and peeled

1. Preheat the oven to 225°. Season the roast with lots of salt and pepper. Slather the meat with butter, working it into the meat. Sprinkle the thyme leaves over the roast.

2. Heat a heavy-bottomed roasting pan over high heat. When it's fully heated, sear the roast on all sides until it turns a luscious brown. Remove the roast and scatter the onions, carrots, potatoes, and garlic in the bottom of the pan. Set the roast on top of the vegetables.

3. Put the pan into the oven and roast, uncovered, for 1 hour and 15 minutes, or until the meat reaches an internal temperature of 125° on a meat thermometer. Transfer the roast to a platter and surround with the potatoes and other vegetables. Let the roast rest for 15 minutes before you carve the meat.

RATATOUILLE
Serves 8

Since we spent time in Provence years ago, I've been in love with this perfect mixture of summer vegetables. Ratatouille is that one dish that I'm happy to serve either hot or cold. The important thing is make sure the eggplant has cooked all the way through to avoid an astringent aftertaste. I add the zucchini and yellow squash as late as possible to retain their crunchy texture and beautiful color.

⅓ cup olive oil	1 yellow squash, diced
1 large eggplant, diced	Salt
1 medium onion, minced	Freshly ground black pepper
1 bell pepper, diced	Leaves from 2 sprigs fresh basil, chopped
4 cloves garlic, minced	
2 tomatoes, chopped	
1 green zucchini, diced	

1. In a large skillet, heat the olive oil over high heat. When the oil begins to shimmer, add the eggplant and cook, stirring frequently, until soft. Lower the heat to medium high and add the onions and bell pepper. Cook until the onions soften, then add the garlic, continuing to stir frequently.

2. Add the tomatoes, lower the heat to medium, and cook for about 10 minutes or until the eggplant has cooked through. Add the zucchini and yellow squash. Taste and season well with salt and pepper. Cook for 3–5 more minutes, until the squash softens. Remove from the heat and stir in the basil.

CAULIFLOWER, ELEVATED: Roasting recasts this humble vegetable from ordinary to knockout. It reappears in Cauliflower Mac & Cheese, page 83. Opposite, Luke is good to the very last drop.

OLIVE OIL–ROASTED CAULIFLOWER
Serves 8

I like to roast the cauliflower in a hot oven until it browns, knowing that it might still be a bit crunchy. But within minutes of removing it from the oven, the florets will noticeably soften. We often eat our roasted cauliflower cold as a snack the next day.

2 tablespoons olive oil	Salt
1 clove garlic, sliced	Freshly ground black pepper
1 head cauliflower, cut into florets	

1. Preheat the oven to 425°. In a bowl, combine all ingredients and toss to coat the cauliflower. Transfer to a baking sheet and roast for 20–25 minutes, until golden brown.

ROSEMARY & GARLIC ROAST FINGERLING POTATOES
Serves 8–10

These are the perfect potatoes for any roast meat. What's important is to make sure the garlic and potatoes roast until they are both tender on the inside, then add the rosemary, crisp the potatoes, and serve immediately.

2 pounds fingerling potatoes, unpeeled	¼ cup olive oil
12 cloves garlic, peeled	Leaves from 2 sprigs fresh rosemary, minced
Salt	
Freshly ground black pepper	

1. Preheat the oven to 375°. Put the potatoes and garlic in a mixing bowl and season with salt and pepper. Drizzle with the olive oil and toss to coat.

2. Transfer the potatoes and garlic to a small ovenproof dish and roast for 15 minutes, or until the potatoes are crusty on the outside and fork tender. Remove from the oven, sprinkle with the minced rosemary, then return to the oven for another 7–10 minutes, to crisp the potatoes.

PERFECT MASHED POTATOES

Serves 10

If you don't already own a good old-fashioned food mill, now's the time to go get one. Potato ricers work fine, but it takes so long to refill the potatoes, the mixture cools down so much that you're liable to overwork the potatoes as you add the butter. A food mill makes mashed potatoes a cinch and is indispensable for making tomato sauce. Good butter matters here!

3 pounds Yukon Gold potatoes, peeled and cut into 1-inch dice	1 pound good quality unsalted butter, diced
	Salt

1. Place the potatoes in a large pot and add enough cold, salted water to cover by 2 inches. Cover and bring to a boil. Lower the heat and simmer for about 30 minutes, until fork tender. Drain in a colander.

2. Using a potato ricer, or preferably a food mill, mash the potatoes (while still hot) back into the pot. Turn the heat to medium low and gently fold the butter into the mashed potatoes. Once the butter is incorporated, season with salt and serve immediately.

STRING BEANS WITH GARLIC

Serves 8

I make sure to have a serving bowl ready with paper-thin sliced garlic and butter just waiting for the hot string beans to arrive. Then all I have to do is boil the beans, toss, and serve. The residual heat from the beans will warm the garlic and melt the butter. I like to salt the water for the beans to the point where it tastes like the sea.

1 pound very fresh string beans, ends trimmed	Salt
	Freshly ground black pepper
2 cloves garlic, thinly sliced	
2 tablespoons butter	

1. Bring a large pot of salted water to a boil. Add the string beans and cook for 3 minutes. Meanwhile, combine the garlic and butter in a serving bowl. Drain the beans and transfer to the bowl. Toss the beans with butter and garlic and season with salt and pepper.

ROAST BEET SALAD
Serves 8

If you can't find the tiny little beets that I like the best, then go ahead and use larger ones. But if you do, please turn the oven temperature down to 350° and obviously let them roast longer—say, an hour. Peel, then cut and toss with the other ingredients.

2	pounds small red and yellow whole beets	1	medium red onion, thinly sliced
½	cup olive oil	½	cup rice wine vinegar
	Salt	2	tablespoons sugar

1. Preheat the oven to 425°. Rub the beets all over with half the olive oil and then salt generously. Place on a baking sheet and roast for 25 minutes. The beets should be soft all the way through.

2. Allow the beets to cool and then peel and cut into quarters. Transfer to a mixing bowl and toss with remaining ¼ cup olive oil, the red onion, vinegar, and sugar. Season with more salt.

CHEESY BAKED POLENTA
Serves 6

This polenta is so good, I sometimes serve it with a big green salad and call it dinner. The quality of the corn is crucial, so try to use organic polenta if you can find it. Resources, page 254.

1	tablespoon olive oil	¼	cup freshly grated Parmesan cheese
4	cloves garlic, sliced	1	cup ricotta cheese
1½	cups polenta		Salt
½	cup shredded fresh mozzarella cheese		Freshly ground black pepper

1. Preheat the oven to 400°. In a large heavy-bottomed pot, heat the olive oil and sliced garlic together over medium heat for about 3 minutes. Raise the heat to high, add 6 cups water, and bring to a boil. Once the water is boiling, slowly add the polenta, whisking rapidly, until the mixture returns to a boil. Cover the pot and lower the heat to a very low simmer. Cook, stirring occasionally, for at least 30 minutes, until the water is absorbed and the polenta is soft.

2. Fold in the three cheeses and season with salt and pepper. Pour the polenta into an ovenproof dish and bake for 20–30 minutes, or until golden brown.

BRUSSELS SPROUTS & BACON
Serves 8

You can easily use olive oil instead of bacon fat for these sprouts. Simply make sure to coat each piece well so the sprouts don't dry out. Use a pan that's large enough so the sprouts aren't piled on top of each other, which ensures that they'll cook evenly.

½	pound bacon, sliced into ½-inch strips		Salt
1½	pounds Brussels sprouts, halved		Freshly ground black pepper

1. Preheat the oven to 450°. In a large ovenproof skillet, cook the bacon over medium heat until cooked through, about 8 minutes. Remove the bacon from the pan with a slotted spoon and reserve. Turn off the heat, add the Brussels sprouts, and stir to coat with bacon drippings.

2. Put the pan in the oven and roast for 10 minutes. Remove the sprouts from the oven. Sprinkle with the bacon and season with salt and pepper.

COUSINS: Brendan, our oldest, cares for Olivia Bourgault, the brand new daughter of Jen's sister, Kim.

SWEET CORN PUDDING
Serves 10–12

The cooking time of this savory pudding will vary greatly depending upon how hot the mixture is when it goes into the oven. You can make the corn mixture up to a day in advance, refrigerate, and then bake just before serving. If you chose to do this make sure to lower the heat to 350° and allow the pudding to bake a bit longer.

8 tablespoons butter	3 tablespoons minced canned jalapeño peppers
1 medium onion, chopped	Salt
2 cloves garlic, sliced	Freshly ground black pepper
12 ears corn, kernels cut off the cob	
¼ cup flour	9 eggs, beaten
1 quart heavy cream	1 cup shredded white Cheddar cheese
1 cup cooked grits	

1. Preheat the oven to 425°. Melt the butter in a heavy-bottomed pot over medium heat. Add the onions and garlic and cook for 3 minutes. Add the corn kernels and cook, stirring, for an additional 3 minutes. Add the flour and stir for 1 minute, then add the cream. Once the cream is incorporated, continue to stir until the mixture comes to a boil. Add the cooked grits, remove from the heat, and stir in jalapeño peppers. Taste and season well with salt and pepper.

2. With a hand-held immersion blender in the pot (or transfer the mixture to a food processor), purée the corn mixture while slowly adding the beaten eggs, until the eggs are thoroughly mixed in.

3. Pour the mixture into an ovenproof dish and sprinkle with the cheese. Bake for 25–30 minutes, until the center puffs and the corn pudding turns golden brown.

SWEET & TART: Brendan and my mother dish over corn pudding. Watermelon pickles are a Southern treat at our restaurant La Provence, where chef Erick Loos makes plenty to sell.

FIELD PEAS

Serves 8

Every region of the country has its version of field peas, called by local names. In New Orleans, we find black-eyed peas, crowder peas, and purple hull peas fresh in season; otherwise, good luck. The next best thing is dried peas. They're all good, but fresh ones have better flavor and cook in half the time. Use these peas in Southern Soup au Pistou (page 93).

2 tablespoons bacon drippings	1 ham hock
1 medium onion, chopped	1 pound fresh field peas, or dried peas, soaked in water overnight
1 clove garlic, crushed	

1. Heat the bacon drippings in a deep heavy-bottomed pot. Add the onions and garlic and cook until soft, about 5 minutes. Add the ham hock and field peas and cover with water (about 1 gallon). Cover, bring to a boil, then lower the heat to a simmer. Cook for 45 minutes to an hour, adding more water if needed, until the peas are tender. Dried peas will take a bit longer. Remove the ham hock to serve.

EGGPLANT DRESSING

Serves 10–12

I like to serve this simple roasted eggplant dish with any roast meat. Add a bit more shrimp and crabmeat, and it becomes the centerpiece of a meal. If you wish to get a jump on this recipe by roasting the eggplants a day ahead and stashing them in the refrigerator, that's a perfectly good idea. Whenever I have a hot oven, I'll throw in a few eggplants and figure out what to do with them later.

2 large eggplants, halved lengthwise	½ pound crabmeat
1 tablespoon olive oil	½ cup bread crumbs
2 tablespoons butter	Leaves from 1 sprig fresh thyme
1 medium onion, diced small	1 dash ground allspice
1 stalk celery, diced small	2 dashes Tabasco
2 cloves garlic, minced	Salt
½ pound medium Louisiana or wild American shrimp, peeled and chopped	Freshly ground black pepper

1. Preheat the oven to 400°. Rub the eggplants with the olive oil and place flesh side down on a baking sheet. Bake for 30 minutes, until soft and almost collapsing. Allow to cool. Once cool, remove and discard the skins. Chop the soft eggplant flesh and reserve in a bowl.

2. Melt the butter a heavy-bottomed skillet over high heat. Add the onions, celery, and garlic and cook, stirring constantly, until softened. Lower the heat to medium, add the eggplant, and cook for an additional 10 minutes.

3. Transfer the eggplant mixture to a large mixing bowl. Add the shrimp, crabmeat, bread crumbs, thyme, allspice, and Tabasco and mix well. Season with salt and pepper, then spoon into an ovenproof dish. Bake at 400° for 30 minutes, or until golden brown.

PROVENÇAL STUFFED TOMATOES

Serves 6–8

I want you to use whatever kind of tomato you can find that's locally grown. I grew up eating our sweet Creole tomatoes, but nowadays I use whatever type we have on our farm. Medium or large, red, yellow, or orange, it makes no difference as long as they're fresh and flavorful.

6 medium or large tomatoes
Salt
Freshly ground black pepper
2 tablespoons plus ½ cup olive oil

½ cup dried bread crumbs
3 tablespoons freshly grated Parmesan cheese
2 cloves garlic, peeled
3 sprigs fresh basil

1. Preheat the oven to 350°. Cut the tomatoes in half width-wise. Place on a baking sheet or in a casserole dish, cut side up, and generously season with salt and pepper. Drizzle with 2 tablespoons of the olive oil.

2. In a food processor or blender, combine the remaining ½ cup olive oil, the bread crumbs, Parmesan, garlic, basil, and 2 pinches of salt and process for about 1 minute. The mixture should have a wet, crumbly consistency.

3. Press the bread crumb mixture onto the tomatoes. Bake for 15 minutes, or until the tops are browned and the tomatoes are warmed through.

chapter three

Dinner from a Cast Iron Pot

"I think of slow-cooked, one-pot meals as country food...

braises, étouffées, fricassees, and stews. No matter what country you're from, you know what I'm talking about—the great French coq au vin (left), the Italian bollito misto, the Spanish suquet—only the names change. What they share is the essence of flavor and the luxury of time that turns meals from those pots into culinary treasures, meals that bring people as well as flavors together. I've promised myself to feed my family and friends as many of these one-pot meals as I can manage.

It's entirely conceivable that one day this treasure of slow-cooking will no longer exist as fewer and fewer folks take up any kind of pot to cook for themselves; as more and more folks become dependent upon fast foods and a whole supermarket full of highly processed and spectacularly unhealthy "dinner options." Oddly, a great many of these same people who never cook consider the act of cooking a high-end sport that takes place on television, not meant for the kitchen at all. Every night we can watch professional cooks, and novices too, in a frenzy of preparation. Or, as in most food television shows, watch them allude to cooking in front of the cameras. It's pure entertainment, and folks are glued to their televisions, munching their plastic-bag snacks that have a list of ingredients as long as your arm.

Please take my preaching with a grain of (sea) salt as I am a self-proclaimed, or rather a self-confessed, hypocrite who has in many ways prospered from the food/television relationship. But I openly admit that this contradiction has helped me see the error of my ways. At one time, after the devastation of Hurricane Katrina had crippled the restaurants of New Orleans, putting suppliers and farmers and growers of all kinds out of business, I gladly took part in cooking competitions on TV because I believed my appearance could help communicate to people all across this country that it was okay, even urgent, to return to New Orleans, to visit or to live.

IN THE MELTING POT: Fresh-picked okra pods ready to mellow a stew, top. How a slow-cooked braise builds flavor, far left, with the inevitable garlic and onion, left. One of our organic roosters is destined for a pot of Coq au Vin, right. Far right, I'm proud of our prized organic chickens, raised in the back of La Provence. She and her friends are the source of the organic yard eggs on our menus.

When I stepped back to ponder that purpose—to help us recover from the massive setback of the storm—I also realized that by doing that kind of TV, I might actually be hurting the same local food culture and family involvement I was seeking to protect. That's what led me to work on the television show *Inedible to Incredible* with Discovery Studios and TLC, where I had the opportunity at last to try to improve the way America cooks—"one ordinary kitchen at a time," as we say on TV. As I traveled and filmed this show, doing "cooking interventions" in the kitchens of people who really needed some help and guidance, it was obvious that what people need now is to be shown the way back to the kitchen, to be encouraged to take the plunge into real cooking.

Which, of course, led me to write **My Family Table**. At last I could act on what I profoundly believe: If we as humans are to continue to evolve as a civilized society, we most certainly must find the time to slow down, to figure out how to make time to cook and eat with each other. This kind of communication is more fulfilling and more satisfying than anything that goes out through the airwaves.

All this is a very long way back to the cast iron pot! This vessel belongs not just to a past where our families once cooked and ate for the sake of sustenance and survival, but to our future as well. No, this is not a 30-minute meal. Instead, it's a meal of considerable investment of time and ingredients with the power to warm the soul and satisfy the palate.

Praise for the Braise

MOST OF MY COOKING POTS at home are heirlooms, passed down to me from generations of folks who really knew how to use them to cook from the heart. If you think about it, until recently few people would ever have had the chance to enjoy choice cuts of meat. Rather, they'd bring home the cheaper, tougher cuts. And how else do you cook rib meat, brisket, shank, neck, or tail than low and slow with moisture—most often with a touch of water, not wine—and a few inexpensive aromatic vegetables like onions and carrots?

The dishes that conjure images of the cast iron pot most certainly were born out of old style localism, where you cooked what you had. Period. I smile at today's fuss about making the perfect stock, or using the right wine to bring out the flavor of meat and vegetables. It used to be that where you lived pretty much dictated whether you'd fricassee a chicken with wine or water. If you think about it that way, today's cast iron pot meals are a sophisticated luxury we can afford.

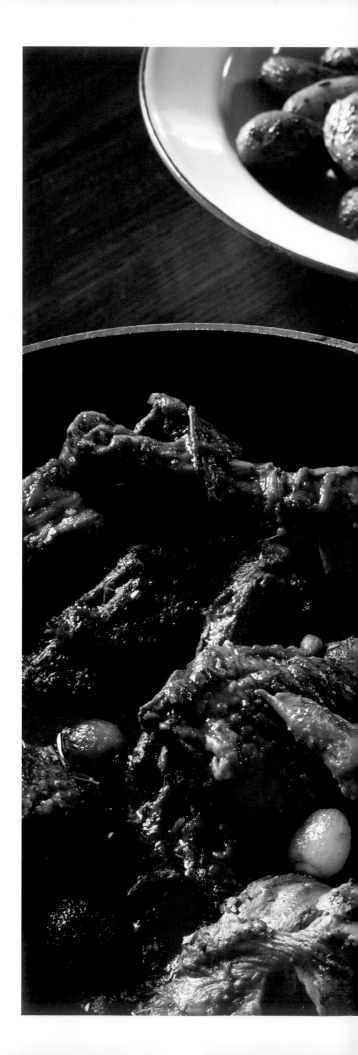

CHICKEN FRICASSEE
Serves 8

The soul of this stew is not that much different from that of the Coq au Vin (page 66). But even though it's just one-pot cooking, you will elevate the chicken in a way that's impossible with any other cooking method. If you take the time to carefully brown the chicken, just a few pieces at a time until they turn crispy, it will intensify the flavor of the dish. If you're tempted to use skinned, deboned chicken, please don't. Not only is the favor brought out by browning with the skin on, but the bone is the source of so much of the deep flavor of the fricassee.

3 tablespoons olive oil	2 quarts chicken broth
2 4-pound free-range, organic chickens, cut into 8 pieces each	8 ounces dried porcini or other wild mushrooms
Salt	Leaves from 2 sprigs fresh thyme
Freshly ground black pepper	1 pound baby carrots, peeled
1 onion, diced	1 pound baby turnips, peeled and diced
4 stalks celery, diced	½ pound small onions peeled
4 cloves garlic, thinly sliced	½ pound fingerling potatoes, halved
1 12-ounce can diced tomatoes	

1. In a large cast iron pot, heat the olive oil over high heat. Add the chicken pieces a few at a time, and brown on all sides. As they brown, season with salt and pepper and transfer to a platter.

2. Add the onions to the pot and cook over moderate heat to soften. Add the celery and garlic and cook until they turn a rich brown, about 5 minutes. Add the tomatoes and cook, stirring, for 3 more minutes.

3. Add the chicken broth, mushrooms, and thyme. Return the chicken to the pot and bring to a simmer. Lower the heat, cover, and simmer for 45 minutes. Add the carrots, turnips, onions, and potatoes. Cover and cook for an additional 30 minutes, or until the chicken is fork tender and the thigh bones are loose.

4. Not surprisingly, I like to serve my fricassee in a shallow bowl over Louisiana rice.

COQ AU VIN

Serves 6–8

When they make coq au vin in France, they'll slow-cook a rooster in the wine. If you can find such a good old bird—an older hen will do—you'll be rewarded with greater depth of flavor. Why is older better? Those birds are tougher and they'll stand up to a long braise far better than common little fryers. If you can't find a bigger bird, use two small chickens (but make sure they're farm-raised, not factory-raised) and don't cook them quite as long. You'll still love the result. I like to marinate the bird overnight.

FOR THE MARINADE

- 1 bottle red wine
- 1 onion, chopped
- 1 carrot, chopped
- 1 stalk celery, chopped
- 2 cloves garlic, crushed
- 3 sprigs fresh thyme
- 1 bay leaf
- ¼ teaspoon black pepper

FOR THE CHICKEN

- 1 6–7-pound rooster or large stewing hen
  Salt
  Freshly ground black pepper

- 2 tablespoons olive oil
- 1 onion, diced
- 1 carrot, diced
- 1 stalk celery, diced
- 2 tablespoons flour
- 1 tablespoon tomato paste
- 1 tablespoon sugar
- 2 cloves garlic, crushed
- 1 quart chicken broth
- 1 12-ounce can diced tomatoes
- 1 bay leaf
  Leaves from 1 sprig fresh thyme, chopped

1. For the marinade, mix all the ingredients together in a large non-reactive bowl.

2. For the chicken, using a sharp knife, cut the rooster or hen into 8 pieces, leaving the bones in. Put the pieces in the marinade bowl. Mix together well, cover the bowl with plastic wrap, and refrigerate for 24 hours.

3. The next day, remove the chicken and pat dry with paper towels. Pour the marinade and vegetables into a cast iron pot and bring to a boil over high heat. Lower the heat to a simmer and reduce the liquid by a third, about 30 minutes. While the marinade is simmering, remove fat and impurities. Strain the marinade and transfer to a bowl to use later.

4. Generously season the chicken with salt and pepper. Wipe out the pot, set it over high heat, and pour in the olive oil. Working in batches, add the chicken pieces and brown them well on all sides. As the pieces brown, remove to a plate.

5. Add the onions, carrots, and celery to the pot and cook, stirring often, until browned. Sprinkle the flour over the vegetables and stir to mix well. Add the tomato paste, sugar, and garlic and reduce the heat to medium. Stirring frequently, cook for 5 additional minutes. Add the chicken broth, diced tomatoes, bay leaf, thyme, and reserved marinade. Cover and bring to a boil. Add the chicken pieces and lower the heat to a simmer. Cook, covered, for 2 hours, or until the chicken is fork tender. Discard the bay leaf.

6. I serve this succulent stew in shallow soup bowls with Louisiana rice or potatoes or pasta to sop up the wonderful chicken juices.

BRAISED VEAL BRISKET

Serves 8–10

Veal brisket, or veal breast as it is more often called in stores, is perfect for slow cooking. But veal breast can be very hard to find, in which case, ask your butcher for a boneless veal neck roast or a roast from the veal shoulder.

1 5-pound veal brisket	1 12-ounce can diced tomatoes
Salt	2 cups beef broth
Freshly ground black pepper	1 cup chicken broth
¼ cup olive oil	2 cloves garlic, minced
2 onions, diced	Leaves from 3 sprigs fresh thyme
1 carrot, peeled and diced	2 bay leaves
1 stalk celery, diced	
3 tablespoons flour	

1. Season the veal all over with salt and pepper. Heat the olive oil in a large cast iron pot over high heat. Add the veal and carefully allow each side to brown, turning often. Remove the veal to a platter.

2. Add the onions, carrots, and celery to the pot. Stir constantly until the onions take on a mahogany color, about 5 minutes, being careful not to let them burn. Sprinkle the flour over the vegetables, mix well, and cook for 3 more minutes. Return the veal to the pot and add the tomatoes, beef broth, chicken broth, garlic, thyme, and bay leaves. Bring to a boil, then reduce the heat and simmer for 1–1½ hours, until the meat is fork tender. Remove the veal to a platter and cover.

3. Reduce the pan liquids by half over medium-high heat. Return the veal to the pot, season with salt and pepper, and heat through. Discard the bay leaves. Transfer the meat to a cutting board and slice. Serve the sauce on the side.

DUCK STEWED WITH APPLES & TURNIPS

Serves 4

Braising a duck is less conventional than roasting it, but the result is wonderful to behold. The Pekin, or Long Island, duck has paler flesh than other ducks and a bit more fat as well. Try to find this larger duck for this stew, as the breasts are more developed and will be more tender.

1 6-pound Pekin duck, cut into 8 pieces	1 celery root, peeled and diced
Salt	1 pound turnips, peeled and diced
Freshly ground black pepper	5 Fuji apples, peeled, cored, and diced
1 teaspoon Chinese five-spice powder	4 cloves garlic, minced
3 tablespoons flour	1 quart chicken broth
1 tablespoon olive oil	2 tablespoons cider vinegar
2 onions, diced	2 tablespoons sugar
1 carrot, peeled and diced	

1. Season the duck pieces all over with salt, pepper, and the five-spice powder. Dust with the flour.

2. In a cast iron pot, heat the olive oil over medium-high heat. Add the duck and brown all over, 2–3 minutes per side. When the skin is crisp, remove the duck to a platter.

3. Add the onions, carrots, celery root, turnips, apples, and garlic to the pot and lower the heat to medium. Cook in the duck fat to soften, 5–7 minutes. We're not looking to brown the vegetables at this point.

4. Add the chicken broth, cider vinegar, and sugar. Bring to a boil. Return the duck legs to the pot, cover, reduce the heat to low, and simmer for about 1 hour. Add the duck breasts and cook for 15–30 minutes more, until the duck meat is fork tender.

5. Stewed duck really must have rice; I have grown fond of Louisiana brown jasmine rice.

BRAISED BEEF SHORT RIBS
Serves 8

I like to use large, fatty beef ribs and cook them on the bone. The bones add more flavor and at the same time ensure that the meat retains its shape. You know the ribs are done when you can pull the meat slowly and easily from the bone.

5	pounds beef short ribs, cut into individual ribs	1	stalk celery, diced
	Salt	2	cloves garlic, crushed
	Freshly ground black pepper	2	tablespoons tomato paste
2	teaspoons dried thyme	2	cups red wine
¼	cup olive oil	1½	quarts beef broth
2	onions, diced	½	pound pearl onions
2	carrots, diced	1	sprig fresh rosemary
		1	bay leaf

1. Season the ribs with salt, pepper, and the thyme. Heat the olive oil in a cast iron pot over high heat. Add the ribs in batches and cook until they're deep brown, 2–3 minutes. Turn the ribs over and brown an additional 2–3 minutes. When they're browned on all sides, remove to a platter.

2. Lower the heat to medium high, add the onions and carrots, and cook until soft. Add the celery and garlic and cook, stirring frequently, until they've turned deep brown, about 5 minutes. Add the tomato paste, continuing to stir frequently, and cook another 3 minutes.

3. Return the ribs to the pot along with the wine, beef broth, pearl onions, rosemary, and bay leaf. Raise the heat and bring to a boil, uncovered. Quickly reduce the heat to a low simmer, cover, and cook for 2–3 hours, or until the meat is fall-off-the-bone tender. Discard the bay leaf and rosemary sprig.

4. Like all braises, short ribs absolutely require a starch to share the juicy wealth such as Perfect Mashed Potatoes (page 51) or Cheesy McEwen Grits (page 104) without the cheese! Serve with browned baby turnips as I do here, if you like.

SLOW-COOKED VENISON
Serves 6

Venison shoulder is the perfect cut for this dish because its lean meat and tough but tasty muscles respond perfectly to a slow braise. If you have difficulty finding a shoulder, use venison shanks instead. They'll need to cook perhaps 30 minutes longer, but they're delicious and worth the wait.

1	4-pound venison shoulder	1	12-ounce can diced tomatoes
	Salt	½	cup dried porcini or chanterelle mushrooms
	Freshly ground black pepper	2	cloves garlic, crushed
¼	cup bacon drippings	3	cups beef broth
2	onions, diced	1	cup red wine
1	carrot, peeled and diced	1	sprig fresh thyme
1	stalk celery, diced	1	sprig fresh rosemary
¼	cup flour	2	bay leaves
			Dash of sugar

1. Season the venison generously all over with salt and pepper. In a cast iron pot, heat the bacon drippings over high heat. Add the venison and sear on all sides until golden brown, 2–3 minutes per side. Remove the venison from the pot and set aside.

2. Reduce the heat to medium. Add the onions, carrots, and celery to the pot and cook until they turn a rich mahogany color, stirring frequently. Add the flour and stir until well combined. Add the tomatoes, dried mushrooms, and garlic. Bring the mixture to a boil and slowly stir in the beef broth and red wine.

3. Raise the heat and bring to a boil. Add the thyme, rosemary, bay leaves, sugar, and venison. Reduce to a low simmer, cover, and cook for about 1½ hours, until the meat pulls easily from the bone. Taste and season well.

4. Transfer the venison to a cutting board and remove the bone. Slice the meat into rough chunks and return to the pot to warm. Discard the herb sprigs and bay leaves.

5. Serve the venison in shallow bowls over Louisiana rice, pasta, or Perfect Mashed Potatoes (page 51).

SEAFOOD-STUFFED CABBAGE

Serves 8

I like this seafood stuffing far better than the usual meat stuffing; it's surprisingly light and refined. If you want your cabbage rolls to look as pretty as ours do, make sure to use Savoy cabbage, then trim the cabbage leaves so they lie flat. Right after you blanch the leaves, lay each leaf, rib side up, on a cutting board and slice off the thick center rib. By removing the excess, you'll be able to roll the cabbage leaves tighter and more uniform-looking.

FOR THE SAUCE

- 2 tablespoons butter
- 2 tablespoons flour
- 1 shallot, chopped
- Leaves from 1 sprig fresh thyme, chopped
- 1 pinch cayenne pepper
- 2 cups seafood broth
- ½ cup white wine
- Salt
- Freshly ground black pepper

FOR THE CABBAGE

- 2 tablespoons olive oil
- 1 onion, diced
- 1 bell pepper, diced
- 2 cloves garlic, minced
- 1 pound small Louisiana or American wild shrimp, peeled, deveined, and chopped
- 2 eggs, lightly beaten
- 1½ cups diced fresh bread
- ½ cup milk
- 2 dashes Tabasco
- 1 pinch celery salt
- 1 pound jumbo lump crabmeat
- 1 head Savoy cabbage, leaves separated

1. Preheat the oven to 325°. For the sauce, melt the butter in a cast iron pot over medium heat until it begins to bubble. Add the flour, whisking briskly until it is thoroughly incorporated. Let the mixture bubble for 1 minute, but don't let it darken. Add the shallot, thyme, and cayenne and continue to whisk as you stir in the seafood broth and wine. Bring the sauce to a simmer and cook until it thickens nicely. Season with salt and pepper. Transfer the sauce to a bowl and refrigerate.

2. For the cabbage, heat the olive oil in a skillet over medium heat. Add the onions, bell pepper, and garlic and sweat until soft. Transfer to a large mixing bowl and mix in the shrimp, eggs, bread, milk, Tabasco, and celery salt. Carefully fold in the crabmeat, keeping the lumps intact. Cool the seafood filling while you blanch the cabbage leaves.

3. Bring a big pot of salted water to boil. Have a large bowl of ice water nearby to cool the leaves as they blanch. Add the cabbage leaves one at a time to the boiling water and blanch for 30 seconds. Transfer to the ice water, then quickly remove from the water and drain flat on towels.

4. Spoon 2 tablespoons of the seafood mixture into the center of each cabbage leaf and roll up burrito-style. Pour the seafood sauce into the bottom of the cleaned cast iron pot. Carefully place each cabbage roll, seam-side down, snugly together over the sauce. There should be enough sauce to rise halfway up the sides of the rolls. Bake, covered, for 20–25 minutes.

School Nights

BLOWING OFF STEAM:
From left, Luke, Jack, Drew, and Brendan in the backyard before dinner.

"A few years back, I made the mistake of questioning my wife…

about what she was feeding our children. She immediately replied that if I was half as concerned about feeding my family as I was about serving my customers, I'd do a better job of helping her with menu ideas that were easy for her to prepare and also happened to be something the lads might actually eat. What she said hit me like a ton of bricks. She was so right. I go to wild extremes to find the perfect fish, the perfect organic grass-fed beef—the perfect anything—for our restaurant guests, but I really

WEEKDAY RITUALS:
Drew (above) can be counted on to provide entertainment while Luke and Jack help Jenifer with their favorite Asian Chicken Salad, opposite above. Another school night, dinner might be as uncomplicated as the best Grilled Ham & Cheese Sandwiches ever, opposite below, to go with Creamy Heirloom Tomato Soup. Lots of feet and lots of flip flops in our house.

wasn't thinking a lot about how to supply my family with similar great foods. During the week, anyway. I was always a Sunday cook—big family spreads, taking my time just cooking and relaxing, doing what I do. But I cook on Sundays as much for me as for them; I spent little time helping Jenifer and the boys manage on those crazy weeknights when I'm nowhere to be found.

The concept of "school night" hardly describes the chaotic schedule my wife keeps throughout the week. Whether school is in session or not, life at the Besh house is a storm of activity. In that way, we're quite the norm—a fact that's made too obvious to me when I'm at the ball park and witness firsthand how many families have dinner from a bag or a box that came from some fast food chain or other.

I am almost never around on weeknights. Even if I'm not at the restaurants, there are football, baseball, and soccer practices and games, which for a dad of four boys you'd imagine would be a lot of fun, and for the most part they were. Until, that is, someone invented travel sports. Now kids don't just play the fellows in the neighborhood, or even the nearby neighborhoods. Now you're driving them out of state on a crazy circuit—as if Luke has already made it to the minors. And he's only eight.

Brendan has an hour commute to school each way, and plays football all around the New Orleans metro area to boot. And that's only two of my boys. Then there's homework and this latest fad of homework for the parents. (You know how it happens—five-year-olds get school projects they couldn't possibly accomplish, so they become parent projects.) And let's not forget civic obligations like fundraisers and boards. It's no wonder families rarely cook and eat together during the week anymore. My challenge was to make that reality better for them, and Jen.

I began to think long and hard about how to solve the problem. I decided that if I gave Jenifer menu ideas that began with what I cook on my Sunday escapades in the kitchen (like roasts), she could prepare simple suppers on weeknights that utilize the kind of Essential Pantry items (page 8) we now try to keep on hand. That way, Jen and the boys can enjoy weeknight suppers that are easy and healthy, and even fun.

Strategies for a School Night

ONE OF THE THINGS that I discovered as a kid and treasure so much as a parent is that food teaches us so much. I love to cook foods from my dear Louisiana, but I also enjoy introducing ingredients and techniques from Vietnam, India, China, Italy, Lebanon, and North Africa into our everyday cooking. The idea is to expose my boys to something interesting and delicious, even if they have to eat it on the run. I figure if I've made the basics available for Jenifer to throw into a hot sauté pan, then she can easily turn out versions of Pad Thai, or pho, or curry over rice. Sunday is our day to sit up straight, eat with utensils, and act like gentlemen; weeknights are for soups to be reheated and simple sandwiches and wraps full of good things.

We joke sometimes about my being so cheap that I'll go to great lengths to figure out how many meals I can make from one chicken. And you know it's true. We chefs must be frugal if there's any hope of getting a return on our investment, and the same should apply at home. To stretch the budget, you've got to get the most out of every ingredient you buy. That's why I love whole chickens, especially organic ones that aren't full of awful hormones and antibiotics. So, when I roast an organic chicken for Sunday supper, I'll use the carcass for a broth or as the base of an incredible soup. Chicken meat pulled off the bone is great in an

Asian Chicken Salad tossed with cabbage and noodles. With a touch of vinegar and hoisin sauce—voila!—two more meals from that one roast chicken.

It's that sort of chef's common sense that I hope to pass along here, making it easier to strategize meals (see Sunday Supper, page 30, for ideas on cooking for the rest of the week). My guys are more excited about eating a sandwich than a salad, so we do wraps, which are a great way to turn a salad into a sandwich. We use tortillas and pita bread, lettuce cups, even dumpling wrappers, anything to build healthy, simple wraps that are fun to eat. We keep tortillas and pitas in the freezer. Pastas are easy for me to cook on Sunday while I've got the whole kitchen messy, so I'll throw on another pot for an extra pound or so. Then, during the week, Jen can turn the pasta into quick pan-fried noodles, reheat it with a marinara sauce, or toss it into a hot broth to make a Vietnamese pho, adding thinly sliced meat and fresh herbs. In this way, soups and salads, pastas and wraps get my family happily and healthily through the week.

CAULIFLOWER MAC & CHEESE

Serves 8

The best thing about this yummy dish is that it comes together so fast. There's only one trick: be sure to add the cheese to the sauce at the last minute and then immediately remove the pan from the heat. If you continue to cook the sauce after adding the cheese, the fats will separate from the proteins and the cheese will become gritty.

1   pound penne pasta
4   tablespoons butter
¼   cup flour
1   quart milk
1   pinch nutmeg
    Salt
    Freshly ground black pepper

1   cup fresh ricotta cheese
⅓   cup shredded Swiss cheese
¾   cup shredded white Cheddar cheese
1   cup or so cooked cauliflower, such as from Olive Oil–Roasted Cauliflower (page 48)

1. Preheat the oven to 375°. In a large pot of boiling, salted water, cook the pasta for 12 minutes, uncovered, then drain in a colander.

2. Melt the butter in a large saucepan over medium heat. Add the flour and cook, stirring constantly, for about a minute, then stir in the milk and bring to a boil. Keep stirring and when the white sauce is well mixed, reduce the heat to simmer. Add the nutmeg and season with salt and pepper.

3. Remove the pan from the heat and stir in the ricotta cheese. Add the pasta and toss well, then stir in the Swiss cheese and half of the Cheddar.

4. Scatter the cauliflower in an ovenproof dish and spoon the pasta and cheesy sauce on top. Smooth the top with a spatula and sprinkle on the remaining Cheddar. Bake for 20–30 minutes, until the cheese is nicely browned.

HEAT & SERVE CHILI
Serves 8

You can use pretty much any roast meat in this chili. Besides brisket, we especially like roast turkey or pork. The beans are interchangeable, too. Cooked lima beans, navy beans, and/or cannellini beans will all work equally well; use what you have. What's important is not to overcook the chili. The meat's been roasted and the beans are ready to go, so think of this as a simple heat-and-serve dish.

1	jalapeño chile pepper	1	carrot, peeled and chopped
¼	cup olive oil		
2	onions, diced	2	teaspoons ground chipotle pepper
1	stalk celery, diced		
2	cloves garlic, minced	1	teaspoon cumin
3	cups chicken broth		Salt
2	cups cooked white beans		Freshly ground black pepper
2	cups roughly chopped cooked meat, such as from Braised Veal Brisket (page 69)	2	green onions, chopped

1. Preheat the oven to 500°. Place the jalapeño on a baking sheet and roast for 10 minutes. Transfer to a small bowl and cover with plastic wrap. When the pepper has cooled, peel away the skin and cut the pepper in half lengthwise. Carefully scrape out the seeds and chop one half. Save the other half for another use.

2. Heat the olive oil in a large saucepan over medium heat. Add the onions and cook until softened, then add the celery and garlic and cook for 5 more minutes. Add the chicken broth, bring to a boil, and then reduce to a simmer.

3. Add the chopped jalapeño, beans, meat, carrots, chipotle, and cumin and return to a boil. Reduce the heat to a simmer and cook until the chili is heated through. Season with salt and pepper.

4. Serve in bowls with green onions scattered on top.

SLOPPY JOE SLIDERS
Serves 8

The sauce for these "any meat" sandwiches is so great, I often make up a batch to keep in the fridge for a few days to use with whatever good braised or roasted meat I have on hand. I make this sauce with my beloved New Orleans staples, Creole mustard and pepper jelly, but it's fine to go ahead and use any good mustard and instead of pepper jelly, add a splash of vinegar to good fruit jam. Slider sauce works beautifully with pork, lamb, or beef. Of course you don't need the onion rings, but their sweet crunch makes all the difference.

FOR THE SLOPPY JOE SAUCE
- 1 teaspoon canola oil
- ½ onion, diced
- 1 cup ketchup
- ½ cup pepper jelly
- ¼ cup rice wine vinegar
- 2 tablespoons honey
- 1 tablespoon Worcestershire sauce
- 1 tablespoon Creole mustard
- Salt
- Freshly ground black pepper

FOR THE SLIDERS
- 2 cups chopped cooked meat, such as from Braised Beef Short Ribs (page 73)
- 16 slider buns, toasted
- Bibb lettuce leaves
- 2 tomatoes, sliced

FOR THE FRIED ONION RINGS
- 2 cups canola oil
- Salt
- 1 cup flour
- 2 red onions, sliced into thin rings

1. For the sauce, heat the canola oil in a saucepan over high heat. Add the onions and cook until browned. Stirring constantly, add the ketchup, pepper jelly, vinegar, honey, Worcestershire, mustard, salt, and pepper and cook until warmed through. Either use immediately, or store in the refrigerator for a few days.

2. For the sliders, warm the sauce in a medium saucepan and add the meat. Stirring well, cook for about 5 minutes, until the sauce and meat are heated through.

3. For the fried onion rings, heat the canola oil in a large saucepan to 350° on a candy thermometer. Mix salt into the flour and spread on a plate. Dredge the onion rings in the flour and drop them, one by one, into the oil. Cook only a few at a time, until the rings are golden. Remove with a slotted spoon and drain on paper towels.

4. Assemble the sandwiches: toast the buns, spoon the saucy meat onto the buns, and top with onion rings, lettuce, and tomato slices.

BEEF NOODLE BOWLS
Serves 6

This is a play on beef noodles, one of my favorite Vietnamese lunches. We make it with chicken, pork, veal, or even shrimp, instead of beef. If the dish seems too spicy, limit the sambal chili paste.

FOR THE SEASONED SAUCE

- ½ cup sugar
- 1 cup seasoned rice wine vinegar
- 2 tablespoons sambal chili paste
- 1 tablespoon fish sauce

FOR THE BEEF

- 3 tablespoons hoisin sauce
- 1 tablespoon sesame oil
- 1 pound Slow-Cooked Beef Chuck Roast (page 47) or raw steak, thinly sliced

FOR THE NOODLES

- 1½ cups pickled daikon, radishes, and carrots (page 25)
- 1 cucumber, thinly sliced
  Mixed baby greens
- 1 pound rice vermicelli noodles, cooked
- 3 green onions, thinly sliced
  Leaves from 1 bunch fresh basil
  Leaves from 1 bunch fresh mint
  Leaves from 1 bunch fresh cilantro

1. For the sauce, bring the sugar, vinegar, chili paste, and fish sauce to a simmer in a small saucepan. Pour in 1 cup of water and stir until the sugar is dissolved. Let cool. Make the sauce in advance and store in the refrigerator.

2. For the beef, in a mixing bowl, combine the hoisin sauce and sesame oil and toss well with the sliced beef.

3. To assemble the bowls, select individual soup bowls deep enough to hold the noodles. In each bowl, combine a few pickled vegetables, the cucumbers, and greens. Divide the noodles among the bowls.

4. Preheat a grill or a large skillet over high heat. Quickly grill or sear the sliced beef. Layer beef slices on top of each noodle bowl and sprinkle with green onions and a few herbs, chopped. Just before serving, drizzle several tablespoons of the seasoned sauce over each bowl. Mix well and enjoy. Put a bowl of the herbs on the table so everybody can add what they like. For spicier noodles, add more chili paste.

ASIAN CHICKEN SALAD
Serves 6–8

Jenifer loves to make this salad with the boys. If there's time, she'll throw it together it a few hours ahead of dinner, but she makes sure to add the herbs at the last minute or they lose the wonderful aromatic qualities that they bring to the salad in the first place. Serve more herbs in bowls for everybody to add as they like.

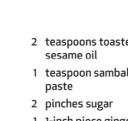

1	head cabbage, thinly sliced
4	3–4 ounce packages dried Ramen noodles, seasoning removed, broken into bite-sized pieces
2	cups or so diced cooked chicken, such as from Herb-Roasted Chicken (page 40)
¼	cup hoisin sauce
3	tablespoons rice wine vinegar
3	tablespoons soy sauce
1	tablespoon fish sauce
2	teaspoons toasted sesame oil
1	teaspoon sambal chili paste
2	pinches sugar
1	1-inch piece ginger, peeled and grated
6	green onions, thinly sliced
¼	cup peanuts, toasted
	Leaves from 1 bunch fresh basil, sliced
	Leaves from ½ bunch fresh cilantro, sliced
	Leaves from 1 bunch fresh mint, sliced

1. Mix together the cabbage, Ramen noodles, and diced chicken in a large bowl. Hands are welcome.

2. In a small bowl or jar, mix the hoisin sauce, vinegar, soy sauce, fish sauce, sesame oil, sambal chili, sugar, ginger, and green onions. Pour over the cabbage mixture and toss really well to coat all the ingredients. You can do this a few hours ahead so that the seasoned sauce will moisten the dried noodles.

3. Just before serving, sprinkle the salad with the peanuts and some of the basil, cilantro, and mint. Have bowls of the herbs on the table so everybody can add what they like.

CHICKEN & NOODLE PAN-FRY

Serves 6

This easy recipe lends itself to endless variations. Sometimes I'll substitute fermented black bean sauce or hoisin sauce for the peanut butter I use here. Or, I'll keep the hoisin and lose the peanut butter. Play around and discover which flavors you prefer. The finished dish looks festive and enticing.

2 tablespoons sesame oil

2 green onions, thinly sliced

1 tablespoon peeled and minced fresh ginger

1 clove garlic, minced

1 cup chicken broth

2 teaspoons rice wine vinegar

1 tablespoon peanut butter

2 teaspoons hoisin sauce

1 tablespoon sambal chili paste

1 pound spaghetti, cooked

Salt

Freshly ground black pepper

2 cups chopped cooked chicken, such as from Herb-Roasted Chicken (page 40)

Leaves from 1 bunch fresh cilantro, chopped

½ lime

1. Heat the sesame oil in a large skillet over high heat and sauté the green onions, ginger, and garlic for a few moments. Add the chicken broth and vinegar. Next add the peanut butter, hoisin sauce, and chili paste. Stir well and bring to a boil.

2. Add the cooked spaghetti and stir well to coat. Lower the heat to medium and season with salt and pepper.

3. Add the chopped chicken and allow to heat all the way through. Transfer to a large serving dish and generously sprinkle with the cilantro. Squeeze the lime over the top.

VIETNAMESE NOODLE SOUP

Serves 6

On almost any night, we love nothing more than a big, hot bowl of Vietnamese noodle soup—pho. Don't worry about the number of ingredients in this recipe. Pho is nothing more than a flavorful broth often perfumed with star anise. Since that's not easy to find, we use Chinese five-spice powder (which has star anise in it). As for the chili paste and hoisin sauce, the Essential Pantry (page 8) is incomplete without these key ingredients.

1 tablespoon sesame oil

4 green onions, chopped

2 tablespoons peeled and minced fresh ginger

2 cloves garlic, sliced

2 teaspoons Chinese five-spice powder

3 quarts chicken broth
  Salt
  Freshly ground black pepper

½ pound rice vermicelli noodles, cooked

1 pound sliced cooked meat, such as from Braised Veal Brisket (page 69)
  Leaves from 1 bunch fresh cilantro
  Leaves from 1 bunch fresh basil

2 limes, quartered

2 handfuls bean sprouts
  Hoisin sauce
  Sambal chili paste

1. Heat the sesame oil in a large heavy-bottomed saucepan over medium-high heat. Add the green onions, ginger, garlic, and five-spice powder and sauté for 2–3 minutes. Add the chicken broth, raise the heat to high, and bring to a boil. Reduce the heat to medium low. Taste and season with salt and pepper and cover the pot.

2. Divide the cooked rice noodles among 6 soup bowls. Over each bowl of noodles, scatter equal portions of sliced meat, then pour the hot broth over the noodles so that the meat is barely covered.

3. In the center of the table put plates of the fresh herbs, lime quarters, and bean sprouts. Each person can add his own fresh herbs and bean sprouts to the soup. Squeeze lime over the top, season with hoisin and chili, stir well, and start slurping.

HEARTY BAKED PASTA

Serves 6

This is a baked pasta for all meats. You can easily substitute pork or chicken for the beef and the recipe will work perfectly. The point is to make it in the morning and bake right before dinner, or even bake it a few days ahead, say on Sunday, refrigerate and reheat when you need a hearty cooked dinner. That's what we do.

3 tablespoons olive oil

1 onion, diced

1 carrot, peeled and diced

2 cups diced cooked meat such as Slow-Cooked Beef Chuck Roast, (page 47) or Braised Veal Brisket (page 69)

2 cloves garlic, thinly sliced

1 tablespoon crushed red pepper flakes

1 teaspoon dried oregano

2 12-ounce cans diced tomatoes

Salt

Freshly ground black pepper

1 pound penne or other shaped pasta, cooked

Leaves from 2 sprigs fresh basil, sliced

1 cup shredded fresh mozzarella cheese

1. Preheat the oven to 400°. In a large heavy-bottomed saucepan, heat the olive oil over medium-high heat. Add the onions and carrots and cook, stirring, until browned, about 10 minutes. Add the beef, garlic, pepper flakes, and oregano, stir for 3 minutes, then add the tomatoes. Raise the heat to high, bring to a boil, then immediately lower to a simmer. Season with salt and pepper.

2. Add the pasta and basil to the pot, stir gently, then pour the contents into a large baking dish. Top with the mozzarella and bake for 10 minutes, or until the cheese has browned a bit. Serve immediately.

SOUTHERN SOUP AU PISTOU

Serves 8–10

This is my idea of the perfect vegetable soup. Notice I didn't say vegetarian, as it does contain a bit of pork and chicken broth. If you wish to use vegetable broth and omit the bacon, then of course do so, and proceed with the recipe with whatever vegetables you have on hand. Using field peas (such as black-eyed peas) makes it Southern, and pistou is the French way with pesto.

FOR THE SOUP
- 1 cup chopped bacon
- 4 cups Ratatouille (page 48)
- 1 cup cooked Field Peas (page 55)
- 1½ quarts chicken broth
- 1 cup string beans, chopped
- Salt
- Freshly ground black pepper

FOR THE PISTOU
- Leaves from 1 big bunch fresh basil
- ¼ cup grated Parmesan cheese
- 2 cloves garlic, minced
- ½ cup olive oil

1. For the soup, cook the bacon in a heavy-bottomed pot over high heat until the fat is rendered. Lower the heat to medium and add the ratatouille, field peas, and chicken broth. Mix well and bring to a boil. Lower the heat to a simmer and add the string beans. Cook for 20 minutes more. Season with salt and pepper to taste.

2. For the pistou, combine the basil leaves, Parmesan, and garlic in a blender and pulse until well mixed. Slowly drizzle in the olive oil, pulsing, until it is all incorporated.

3. To serve, portion the soup into bowls and top each with a heaping tablespoon of pistou.

OUR ITALIAN WEDDING SOUP

Serves 6

This is our Southern interpretation of Italian Wedding Soup, a combination of hearty ingredients that marry together happily. It's a soup substantial enough to be a meal in itself.

- 1 pound Italian sausage, casings removed
- 1 spoonful bacon drippings
- ½ onion, diced
- 1 clove garlic, sliced
- 1 teaspoon crushed red pepper flakes
- 2 quarts chicken broth
- 1 cup chopped tomatoes
- 1 handful chopped mustard or turnip greens
- 1 teaspoon dried oregano
- 4 cups or so cooked black-eyed peas (see Field Peas, page 55)
- Salt
- Freshly ground black pepper

1. Wet your hands a bit and roll the sausage meat into small meatballs. Heat the bacon drippings in a large heavy-bottomed saucepan over medium-high heat. Sear the meatballs quickly in the bacon fat, so that they are well-browned, then add the onions, garlic, and pepper flakes. Cook a few minutes more until the onions soften and the meatballs are cooked through.

2. Add the chicken broth, tomatoes, mustard greens, and oregano and bring to a boil. Add the black-eyed peas and cook until the soup is hot. Taste and season well with salt and pepper.

3. Divide the meatballs among 6 soup bowls and ladle soup into each bowl. Serve with cornbread.

EASY PORK GRILLADES

Serves 6

Grillades—slices of meat slow-cooked like pot roast—are a favorite in our house, but you can make grillades fast using slices of Sunday's pork roast, or uncooked pork, beef, or veal. In that case, you'd slice the meat into thin cutlets, dredge in flour, then brown in olive oil until cooked through. Grillades are great for making ahead of time and then reheating when the family finally arrives home. I love to serve them over Cheesy Baked Polenta (page 52).

- 6 cooked cutlets such as from Slow-Roasted Pork Shoulder (page 38), Pork Rib Roast (page 45), or other meat
- Salt
- Freshly ground black pepper
- 1 teaspoon dried thyme
- ¼ cup olive oil
- 1 onion, diced
- 1 clove garlic, minced
- ¼ cup flour
- 1 cup diced tomatoes
- 1 teaspoon crushed red pepper flakes
- 2 cups chicken or beef broth
- Leaves from 1 sprig fresh oregano, chopped

1. Season the pork cutlets with salt, pepper, and thyme. Heat the olive oil in a large skillet over high heat. In batches, add the cutlets and sear well, browning on both sides. As they brown, remove the cutlets to a platter.

2. Add the onions to the skillet and cook, stirring, for about 7 minutes, or until browned. Add the garlic, dust the vegetables with flour, and stir for 3 more minutes over high heat. Add the tomatoes and red pepper flakes. Bring to a boil and add the broth and oregano. Return to a boil, stirring constantly. Taste and and season well with salt and pepper.

3. Return the pork to the skillet with the sauce. Reduce the heat to low, and cover. Let simmer for at least 5 minutes. Serve a generous portion of polenta on each plate and top with the grillades and lots of gravy.

CREAMY HEIRLOOM TOMATO SOUP WITH GRILLED HAM & CHEESE

Serves 8

The secret to the best tomato soup is to make a tomato sauce when good fresh tomatoes are in season and freeze it to use later for soup—and in any number of other recipes. To make this soup, just pull a container of tomato sauce from the freezer (or open a can of good tomatoes), add a little cream, and you're done. As for the ham, after you've baked and enjoyed your Sunday ham, slice it and freeze it for later. (And if it came with a bone, make sure to save it with any stray bits of ham to cook up in a pot of beans.)

FOR THE SOUP
- ¼ cup olive oil
- 3 cloves garlic, crushed
- 2 12-ounce cans good tomatoes, or 2 quarts Cherry Tomato Five-Minute Sauce (page 26)
- 1 cup organic heavy cream
- 1 teaspoon sambal chili paste
- 1 teaspoon sugar
- Leaves from 3 sprigs fresh basil
- Salt

FOR THE SANDWICHES
- 16 thick slices good white or wheat bread
- Dijon mustard
- 16 slices Swiss cheese
- 16 slices cooked ham, such as from Pecan-Baked Ham (page 42)
- 4 tablespoons butter, plus more as needed

1. For the soup, heat the olive oil in a large, heavy-bottomed saucepan over high heat. Add the garlic and stir for a minute but don't let it brown. Add the tomatoes, cream, chili paste, sugar, and basil and bring to a boil. Transfer to a blender and purée. Season with salt and a pinch more sugar. Keep the soup warm until the sandwiches are ready.

2. For the sandwiches, coat one side of each slice of bread with mustard. Layer the ham and cheese on 8 of the slices, then top with the remaining bread. Melt the butter in a large skillet over medium heat. Add the sandwiches in batches and brown on each side, adding more butter to the skillet as needed. Slice the sandwiches and serve with the tomato soup.

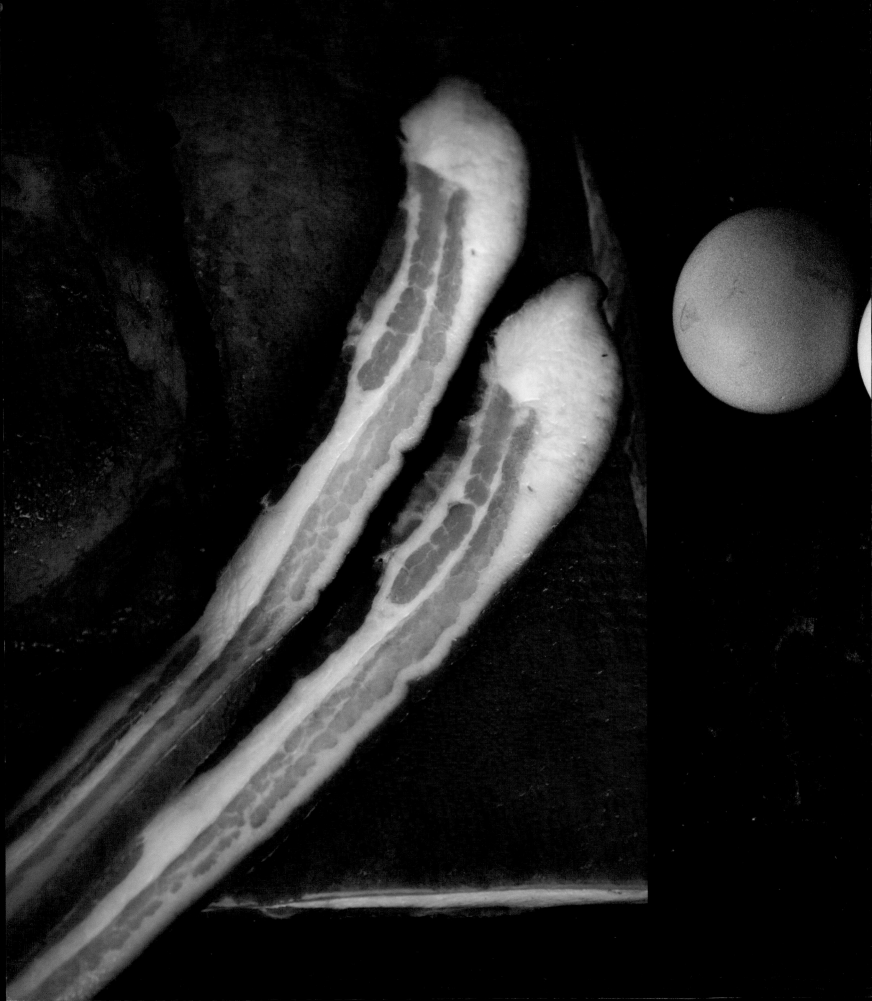

"I smell breakfast in my mind…

It's an Alabama morning and from my sleepy bed I hear my Grandmother Grace in her kitchen and catch the scents of biscuits in the oven, strong dark coffee with chicory in a French drip on the burner, and a cast iron panful of rendered bacon fat—perfuming the entire house. I can't smell the eggs, but I hear them snap and crackle in the hot bacon fat. Without seeing her, I know Grace is spooning simmering bacon fat over the tops of the eggs because she knows that's how I like them. The gentle clanking of metal against glass alerts me to the unscrewing of quince, pear, fig, or scuppernong

SHORT-ORDER DAD:
On special mornings I'll turn out Bird's Nest Potatoes, above. Drew's been into his sunny-side up eggs, right. Opposite, I make bacon on a baking sheet in the oven; Jack loves a good watermelon; plump sausages.

preserves, just waiting to be slathered over the hot, buttery biscuits soon to be freed from the oven. A soft plumping sound tells me that farmers' butter has been unrolled from its wax paper and onto a wooden cutting board, to be sliced and stirred into a large pot of steaming hot grits, making them even creamier.

A faint whiff of tobacco tells me Grandmother's cigarette is slowly smoldering in an ashtray as she works; two puffs on the cigarette and she'll let it go out. She's too busy caring for us to stop and indulge her simple pleasure. This is my idea of culinary ecstasy: orange juice in a Mason jar, a hearty "Good morning John, angel," followed by a "What can I get you for breakfast?" which is then always followed by "You can have anything you want as long as it doesn't hurt you."

A lump forms in my throat at those memories of a loving Grace and her heartfelt cooking. Through her, I came to realize the importance, if not the nobility, of cooking for and serving others, especially those you love. So it's no surprise that one of my most cherished pleasures today is to cook breakfast for my boys. As a chef, I very seldom have the opportunity to be that typical father who is able to spend time in the evenings with the lads, so I figure if I'm to have any quality time with them, it has to be early morning. I happen to be a morning person, which Jenifer certainly is not, so the arrangement works out just fine. Like my own memories of breakfast with my grandmother, I guess I'm hoping my mornings with the boys will be considered a gift that remains with them when they have families of their own.

For this morning ritual I feed them a fine Southern breakfast, hoping to nourish their souls as well as their bodies. Sure there are healthier options, but opening a box of cereal—whole-grain, organic, or what-ever—demands no sense of commitment; it doesn't engender memories. Yogurt might be a better source of protein, but does it feed the imagination like a fluffy stack of pancakes can? Instead, I choose the route of stone-milled grits and fresh eggs from our chicken coop, often cooked in the fat of our own bacon, stored, like my grandmother's, in a jar near the stove.

On a good day (which means everything goes as planned), I like to roll my biscuits out and bake them in the same oven that I cook my bacon. With meat from the neck of our Mangalitsa pigs, ground and seasoned with crushed peppers and cane syrup, sometimes I'll make sausage patties that fit perfectly on a biscuit, the way Jack likes it.

Breakfast with the boys begins with black coffee for me and an oven preheated to 400°; I fill a saucepan with a quart of water for the grits and set it over a high flame. While I wait for the water to boil, I pull out two baking sheets, lay sliced bacon on one and slide it into the oven. If I had the chance to mix the biscuit dough the night before, I would have added a touch of yeast so that they'd rise a bit overnight, so I check on them in the fridge. These I call Angel Biscuits, for Grandmother Grace. Or, I'll make the dough for quick Drop Biscuits. The water is boiling, so I stir in a cup of grits, and then I remove the bacon from the oven, pouring the fat into a Mason jar.

Now it's time to drop the biscuits onto the baking sheet and slide it into the oven for 15 or 20 minutes and to start calling the boys. I stir the grits again, add some cheese and butter, then call a second time, yelling: "Good morning, boys. It's me, your daddy. Rise and shine, give God your glory." After this performance, the lads begin to appear and I start working on the eggs: scrambled for Brendan, over easy for Jack, sunny-side up for Drew, and for Luke an extra biscuit.

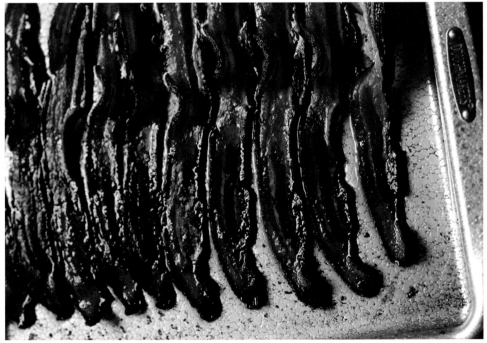

How to Cook an Egg

IT'S SAID THAT THE TRUE WAY to judge a chef is by the way he cooks an egg. I'll admit that egg cooking has been a bit of a sore spot for me ever since that show on Bravo's "Top Chef Masters" where I was given the seemingly simple task of cooking six eggs with one hand tied behind my back. I decided on shirred eggs, each in a ramekin in the oven. Well, to make a long story short, I failed. Sure, the oven did lose power halfway through the process, but it goes to show that cooking eggs can be daunting. Eggs are so common, we take it for granted that we know how to cook them!

To cook an egg, first find a good one. Good eggs come from healthy hens that are allowed plenty of space to grub around for a varied diet of insects and grains, not overcrowded and thus so disease-prone they need to be shot up with antibiotics. Organic nutrients matter here; insuring that hens produce strong shells and firm yolks that will stand tall. You can find good eggs like these at your local farmers' market. We're lucky to get our yard eggs from the organic chickens we raise behind La Provence.

Sunny-side up eggs require a small skillet (size matters), at room temperature, rubbed with good butter. Crack the eggs into the pan over medium-low heat; cook until the yolk becomes warm to the touch. For the good ole' Southern fried egg, we put a healthy spoonful of bacon drippings in the pan and cook the egg over medium heat until the whites coagulate, spooning some of the hot bacon drippings over the yolk to cook the top. Only when the yolk has cooked do we turn the egg over, thus reducing the risk of breaking the yolk. Once flipped, we cook the egg another 30 seconds for over easy, or a minute for over medium.

For scrambled eggs, break a couple of eggs into a mixing bowl, add a shot or two of whole milk and a touch of salt, and whisk violently for a moment. Preheat a small skillet over medium high for a minute or two, add some good butter, and swirl it around so that the entire bottom of the pan is thoroughly coated. Pour out any excess butter before adding the eggs. (If the pan is too hot, the butter won't just melt, it'll brown and you don't want that.) Let the pan cool for a brief moment, wipe it out with a paper towel, and repeat the butter process. Add the eggs, reduce the heat to medium, and stir with a heat-resistant spatula. You're looking to form long curds of cooked eggs over the bottom of the pan. Continue for another minute or so until the eggs are done to your liking. I prefer them on the soft side.

For an omelette, beat the eggs as you would for scrambled eggs, but omit the milk. When you pour the beaten eggs into the twice-buttered pan, stir them faster, thus forming smaller curds of cooked eggs. Continue until the eggs have cooked about halfway through. Then add the cheese or other filling on top of the eggs. Allow the eggs to rest away from the heat for a moment so they've finished cooking, then tilt the pan downward and use the spatula to roll the omelette over and onto a plate.

For boiled eggs, place the eggs in a saucepan and cover with a couple of inches of lukewarm water. Bring the pan to a simmer over high heat. Cover and remove the pan from the heat and let sit for 5 minutes for the perfect soft-boiled egg, 7 minutes for hard-boiled. Once the eggs are cooked, place the pan in a sink and run cold water over the eggs. For warm soft-boiled eggs, remove the eggs from the cool water and enjoy.

For poached eggs, place a saucepan of water on the stove and salt it to your taste. Add a teaspoon of white vinegar for every cup of water. Bring the water to a very low simmer and carefully crack the eggs into the pan. Let the eggs simmer for 3 minutes, then remove them from the water with a slotted spoon.

SIMPLE CHEESE OMELETTE
Serves 2

Feel free to fill the omelette with just about anything you can imagine. But make sure your filling is not cold: too often people add cold meats and vegetables and try to overcompensate by overcooking the eggs. The trick is to warm the filling a bit before adding it to the eggs. Cheese is a different story, as it doesn't take much heat to melt it. Any cheese you have on hand will be wonderful in an omelette.

1 teaspoon olive oil	Freshly ground black pepper
4 eggs, beaten	¼ cup grated or crumbled cheese
Salt	

1. Make sure to have all of your ingredients ready to go and near the stove. Heat the olive oil in a small skillet over medium-high heat. Season the beaten eggs with salt and pepper.

2. Pour the eggs into the skillet, stirring faster than for scrambled eggs, forming small curds of cooked eggs. Continue stirring until the eggs have cooked about halfway through. Then add the cheese or other filling on top of the eggs.

3. Allow the eggs to rest away from the heat for a moment to cook further, then tilt the pan downward and use the spatula to roll the omelette over and onto a plate.

ANDREW'S FRIED EGGS

Serves 1

I've taught Andrew the trustiest way to check on the temperature of the yolk as it cooks: use the back of your finger, which is actually quite sensitive to heat. Barely touch the yolk; if it's warm, it's done.

1	teaspoon butter		Freshly ground black pepper
2	eggs		
	Salt		

1. Heat the butter in a small skillet over medium-low heat. Add the eggs and cook slowly until the whites coagulate and the yolks are heated through. Slide onto a plate and salt and pepper well.

LOU'S SPECIAL

Serves 4

Lou Sedacek was Jenifer's grandfather, a near mythical man from Czechoslovakia who fought in the First World War. According to family lore, Lou made these eggs during the war in a heavy cast iron pan he carried into the field. Everyone in Jenifer's family claims to make the authentic version. Don't worry about having stale bread, what's important is that the bread is dry enough to absorb more of the bacon fat and eggs. Great bacon makes all the difference, see Resources, page 254.

8	slices bacon, diced		Freshly ground black pepper
8	slices stale white bread, cubed		Salt
4	eggs, beaten		

1. Brown the bacon in a skillet over medium heat and pour off fat. Add the cubed bread and brown, stirring frequently, about 3 minutes. Pour the eggs over the bread and cook, stirring constantly, until the eggs begin to firm. Add pepper and a pinch of salt. Serve it up from the pan.

CHEESY McEWEN GRITS

Serves 6

Frank McEwen is a good friend, philosopher, and corn miller who makes the finest grits and cornmeals out of simply the best organic corn, period. If you don't have access to any of his fine products (see Resources, page 254), make sure your grits are stone ground, yielding fine particles along with coarser granules, and you'll have super-creamy grits with great texture.

1	cup McEwen & Sons organic stone ground grits	¼	cup shredded Cheddar cheese
4	tablespoons butter		Salt
			Freshly ground black pepper

1. Bring 1 quart water to a boil in a medium pot over medium-high heat. Stir in the grits briskly and return to a boil. Lower the heat to a simmer (the grits should bubble occasionally) and cook for 20–30 minutes, stirring from time to time. Remove from the heat and stir in the butter and cheese. Continue stirring until the butter and cheese are fully incorporated. Season with salt and pepper.

ANGEL BISCUITS

Serves 12

This is my idea of the perfect light breakfast biscuit (right), but only if you have time to make the dough the night before and let it rise overnight. What's special about these biscuits is what I call a three-way flip: roll the dough out into a rectangle, then fold two opposite sides in so you have a triple fold, making three flaky layers. Cut the biscuits out of the trifold dough, and put them on a nonstick baking sheet and into the refrigerator overnight. In the morning, pop the pan into a preheated oven.

1	package active dry yeast	1½	teaspoons salt
5	cups all-purpose flour	2	cups buttermilk
¼	cup sugar	1	cup (2 sticks) butter
2	tablespoons baking powder		

1. Dissolve the yeast in ¼ cup warm water. Sift together the flour, sugar, baking powder, and salt in a large mixing bowl. Add the buttermilk and dissolved yeast and mix well. Using a pastry knife, cut the butter into the mixture.

2. Since this makes a light, fairly wet dough, sprinkle ½ cup of flour on the counter before you roll out the dough. Roll out the dough into a rectangle. Fold the two sides in, making a triple layer of dough. Cut the dough into 3-inch circles or squares. Place on a nonstick baking sheet, cover loosely, and refrigerate overnight.

3. The next morning, preheat the oven to 400°. Bake for 15–20 minutes, until golden brown.

DROP BISCUITS

Serves 6

Here's my last-minute go-to biscuit recipe, great if I've not prepared Angel Biscuits the night before.

2	cups flour	1	pinch salt
1	tablespoon baking powder	5	tablespoons butter
1	pinch sugar	1¼	cups milk

1. Preheat the oven to 400°. Sift together the flour, baking powder, sugar, and salt in a large mixing bowl. Using a fork, cut the butter into the mixture. Stir in the milk and mix gently until the dough comes together.

2. Drop the dough onto a baking sheet by spoonfuls, leaving enough space between each biscuit for them to expand. Bake for 10–12 minutes, until the biscuits are golden brown.

CRAB-BOIL HOME FRIES

Serves 6

Red bliss potatoes are our favorites to use in crawfish, crab, and shrimp boils, and they're too deliciously seasoned not to fry them up again in the morning for breakfast. Of course we may not have these luscious already-cooked potatoes on hand, so the point here is to spice up parboiled potatoes with crab boil flavors and pan-fry them in bacon fat. What's not to like?

4 red bliss potatoes, unpeeled and quartered	¼ cup bacon drippings
2 tablespoons Zatarain's Crab Boil seasonings or Old Bay seasoning	2 green onions, green parts diced

1. Rinse the potatoes and put in a saucepan with cold water to cover by 2 inches. Add the seasoning and bring to a boil. Reduce to a simmer and cook until the potatoes are fork tender, about 15 minutes.

2. Drain the potatoes and allow them to cool. After 30 minutes, heat about 2 tablespoons of the bacon drippings in a skillet over medium heat. Add half of the potatoes and cook, turning, until golden brown. Transfer to a platter. Repeat with the remaining bacon fat and potatoes. When all the potatoes are cooked, sprinkle with the green onions and serve.

BIRD'S NEST POTATOES

Serves 6

Shredding the potatoes for these super-crunchy "nests" is made easy with a clever device called a Benriner Turning Slicer, or use a heavier Japanese mandoline like the one I'm using below. If I have extra potatoes, I'll make more nests than I need and only cook them halfway. I can then freeze them— first on a nonstick baking sheet, then into a Ziploc bag for longer storage in the freezer. When I want easy potato nests, I take them out and finish cooking them in a lightly oiled skillet. Bird's Nest Potatoes are too good to serve only at breakfast. Make them for dinner, too!

4 russet potatoes, peeled
Salt
½ cup olive oil

1. Shred the potatoes with a spiral turning device, mandoline, or the shredder attachment of a food processor. Lightly salt the potatoes.

2. Heat a generous tablespoon of the oil in a small nonstick skillet over low heat. With a spatula, press enough shredded potatoes into the pan to cover the bottom. Cook slowly until the nest is brown on the bottom, then turn over and cook until the other side is well browned. Drain on paper towels. Repeat until all the potatoes are used.

BUTTERMILK BLUEBERRY PANCAKES

Serves 6

Look, it's totally cool to have lumps in your pancake batter! If you don't, it means you've mixed it too much and the pancakes will turn out a bit tough as a result.

2	cups flour	2	cups milk
⅓	cup sugar	½	cup (1 stick) butter, melted
1	tablespoon baking powder	1	cup blueberries
1	teaspoon salt		Oil for the griddle
2	eggs, beaten		Maple syrup

1. Preheat the oven to 200°. In a large mixing bowl, stir together the flour, sugar, baking powder, and salt. Make a well in the dry ingredients and add the eggs, milk, and melted butter and mix together gently. There will be lumps in the batter. Add half of the blueberries.

2. Lightly oil the surface of a griddle or large skillet and heat over medium heat. Pour ¼ cup of the batter onto the griddle. Continue to pour out pancakes, spacing them well. Cook each pancake until bubbles form on the surface, then turn over and cook for an additional minute. Keep the pancakes warm on a platter in the oven until you've made the whole batch.

3. Serve the pancakes with maple syrup and top with the remaining blueberries.

BROWN BUTTER & VANILLA WAFFLES

Serves 6

You certainly don't need to make the batter a day ahead, but honestly it will work better if you do; a natural fermentation takes place that allows the batter to develop a yeasty flavor. Also, I don't have time in the morning to measure out the ingredients for the batter, so it's so much more convenient to have it ready when I get up. If there's no waffle iron at hand, feel free to turn this batter into pancakes.

½	cup (1 stick) butter, plus more for the waffle iron	½	teaspoon salt
1¾	cups flour	2	eggs, beaten
⅓	cup sugar	2	cups buttermilk
1	tablespoon baking powder	1	teaspoon vanilla

1. A day ahead, cook the butter in a small saucepan over medium heat, stirring, until the aroma is delicious and the color is a rich mahogany. Remove the pan from the heat and reserve.

2. In a large mixing bowl, sift together the flour, sugar, baking powder, and salt. Make a well in the dry ingredients and add the eggs, buttermilk, and vanilla. Then add the browned butter and stir together to combine well. Cover the bowl and refrigerate overnight if possible.

3. The next morning, butter a waffle iron and heat up. Ladle in the batter and cook in batches until the waffles are golden and crisp. Serve immediately.

STUFFED FRENCH TOAST
Serves 8

Nutella is a chocolate hazelnut spread in a jar, created in Italy in the 1940s. When we were living in Europe we became hooked on it. But the truth is, I'll stuff French toast with anything, from peanut butter and honey to apricot preserves, and it's always a hit.

1	13-ounce jar Nutella
16	slices good white bread (or 2 slices per person)
6	eggs, beaten
1	cup milk
½	cup sugar
¼	cup orange juice
4	tablespoons butter, melted
½	teaspoon vanilla
1	pinch salt
¼	cup canola oil

1. Spread 1 tablespoon of Nutella between 2 slices of bread, forming 8 sandwiches. Use the dull edge of a large water glass to cut one clean circle out of each sandwich, cutting off the crusts and sealing the sandwich.

2. Mix together the eggs, milk, sugar, orange juice, butter, vanilla, and salt in a large shallow bowl. Dip the sandwiches in the egg mixture until they are well-covered. Do this in small batches, because you'll cook the French toast immediately after each egg dip.

3. Heat 2 tablespoons of canola oil on a griddle or in a large skillet over medium heat. Add half the sandwiches and cook, turning once, until browned on both sides. Repeat with the remaining oil and sandwiches. Serve immediately.

chapter six

How to Cook a Fish

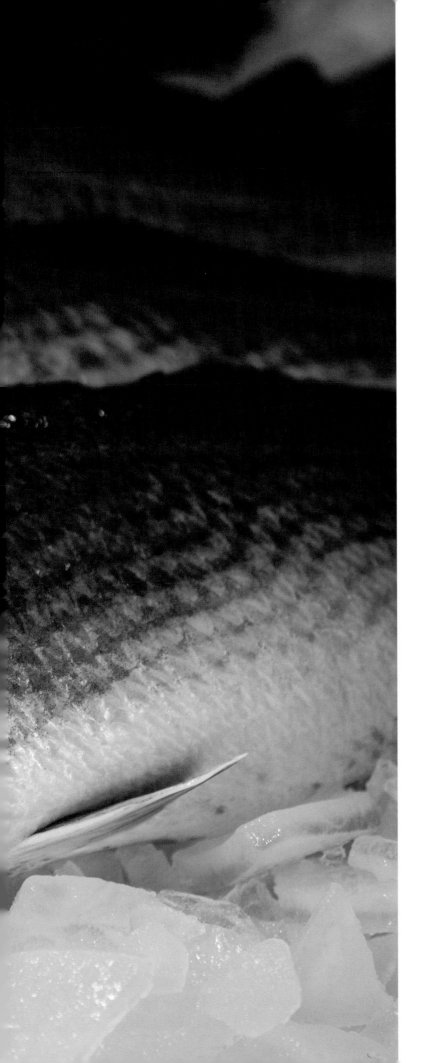

"Growing up in South Louisiana, it never once occurred to me to hate the oil companies…

Offshore oil drilling rigs have been out there in the Gulf my entire life, becoming reef systems for every type of sea creature you can imagine. Going fishing as a child meant heading out to the rigs. Inland rigs attracted redfish and trout for courtbouillon and amandine. A little farther out, it was lemonfish, grouper, and amberjack: fish for the grill. Farther out still were tuna, bull dolphin, wahoo, and other powerful fish just waiting to be caught and

eaten. Oil rigs were our salvation if the boat motor went out on you, or when a massive thunderstorm blew in and trapped you offshore.

Never did I question drilling or oil in general, in part because it was the livelihood of most of the men in our neighborhood; they worked offshore as divers, helicopter pilots, and midlevel management types. We also lived among shrimpers, fishermen, and crabbers. I grew up shrimping with very small trawls I'd pull around the lake with my 15-foot skiff. And every now and then I'd get work as a hand on a big, 65-foot trawler in the Gulf. In between drags, after we sorted and picked the shrimp from the hundreds of other critters that would be swept up in the nets, we'd boil shrimp in a huge pot on a big propane burner. I can still taste those shrimp today—the best I've ever had—boiled by men who took great pride in what they cooked.

Then, on the eve of Earth Day, April 20, 2010, all hell broke loose. BP's Deepwater Horizon rig, some 40 miles out in the Gulf of Mexico, exploded, killing riggers and sending millions of gallons of oil into our precious waters. For 86 days that oil continued to flow, unstoppable, like some dark force erupting from the center of the earth. I was truly sickened by Washington's slow response to the plight of our fishermen, to the threat to our fragile ecosystem, and to the rupture of a whole way of life along our coastline.

I believed we had to hold oil companies responsible. But first we had to protect the citizens and wetlands that have been a crucial source of seafood production for our entire country. I spoke out every chance I got, on television and radio and in print, on behalf of the seafood industry, and the hospitality industry, too. My position was pretty much summed up in an opinion piece I wrote online for the Atlantic Food Channel: "Those of us here are left with a seemingly insurmountable mess, with the richest wetlands of America and a culture to match hanging in

MASTER FISHMONGER:
Brian Cappy, above, my old friend and trusted purveyor, knows good fish and sells them at Kenney's Seafood (see Resources, page 254), below and opposite bottom. Loyal Schatzi supervises grilling salmon, opposite above, as I salt and season a filet with fresh tarragon, left.

the balance. Whoever is looking to assign blame . . . is overlooking the plight of those fish, birds, and people who depend upon the salt marsh estuaries that give the Gulf of Mexico and much of America life. Our wetlands and culture are at stake! Now let us see what we are going to do about it."

The well was sealed for good on July 15, 2010, but the long-term effects are not easily evaluated, given the scope of the spill. I still feel a moral obligation to support and help the fishermen, shrimpers, and crabbers by consuming the fruits of their local labors. Seafood from the Gulf is tested and it is safe. You can be sure I would not serve anything to my family or in my restaurants that I did not know to be perfect.

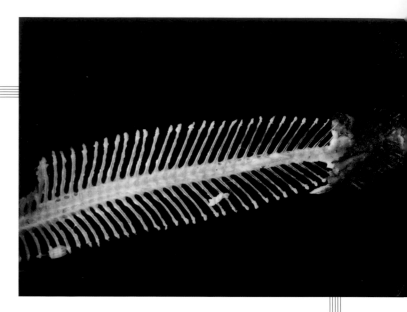

Close to the Bone

IN MY PRETEEN YEARS, I earned the money for bait and fishing tackle by cutting grass in the yards around the block. My friends and I would get one of our mothers to drop us off on the shore of Lake Pontchartrain, where we'd fish all day—for trout and redfish mostly, but inevitably we'd catch sheepshead, flounder, croaker, drum, garfish, pinfish, needlefish, gafftop, channel cats, sand sharks, lake runners, white trout, and even jackfish, which we called Hawaiian tuna. Mom would allow me to cook whatever we caught and that's just what I'd do.

Even at this young age, I had mastered the art of filleting. Whatever the fish, I somehow knew instinctively the proper way to cook it. Okay, I was very young and somewhat hardheaded, but I had paid close attention to the way Mom, Mr. BJ, Mr. Mike, and the rest of them cooked fish or talked about cooking fish. So of course I knew everything.

Sheepshead? Wrap it in cheesecloth and boil it up slowly in water flavored with Zatarain's Crab Boil. I'd fillet garfish and turn it into fish balls that you really needed a food processor to make, but nobody back then had even heard of a contraption like that, so I'd painstakingly chop it by hand. Every other fish I'd fry and turn into a white bread sandwich with plenty of Blue Plate mayonnaise, Creole tomatoes, and Tabasco sauce. Or I'd serve 'em fried on a plate with my special made-up blender version of hollandaise.

Today I'm a wise enough to know there's a whole lot more to cooking fish well than this. People can be funny about cooking fish at home. I can think of two reasons: compared to meat, fish is highly perishable. And folks have a tendency to cook fish like it is meat, which means they seriously overcook it. Wrong! Fish is delicate and subtle, and cooking must be, too. Cooking fish properly starts with a first-rate fishmonger. This is where relationships really matter. A fishmonger you trust will always sell you what's fresh and can skin, scale, and portion the fish for you, thus removing a lot of intimidating guesswork from the process.

Here are a few of my basic fish thoughts:
- White flaky fleshed fish like flounder and sole are great for the sauté pan, dredged in seasoned flour and cooked quickly in oil or butter over high heat.
- I usually cook meaty fish like salmon, tuna, and amberjack on the grill, like meat.
- I always cook fish small enough to cook whole, like sole and freshwater panfish, on the bone, because that's where the flavor is.
- I prefer clear, bright sauces like fruity vinaigrettes and fragrant broths to flatter the flavor of fish cooked very simply.

A DELICATE TOUCH: Taking great care is the secret to great fish cookery. Here, I remove a trout filet from its gentle poaching liquid.

HERB-GRILLED WILD ALASKAN SALMON
WITH BUTTERMILK DRESSING

Serves 8

If it is not wild salmon, do not serve it. That's my simple rule. I just don't trust farm-raised or genetically modified salmon. I don't know of any salmon better than the fatty, rich Alaskan king salmon. It's an impressive centerpiece on the dinner table. Place it on a platter and serve with the chilled Buttermilk Dressing and crispy salad leaves for a perfect summer family meal.

FOR THE SALMON

- 1 2–3-pound skin-on wild Alaskan salmon filet
  Sea salt
  Freshly ground black pepper
- ¼ cup olive oil
- 1 big handful fresh mixed herbs (dill, fennel, chives, tarragon)
  Juice of 1 lemon

FOR THE BUTTERMILK DRESSING

- 1 cup buttermilk
- 1 cup mayonnaise
- ½ cup sour cream
- ¼ cup rice wine vinegar
- 1 tablespoon garlic powder
- 1 tablespoon onion powder
- 1 tablespoon celery salt
- 2 dashes Tabasco
  Salt
  Freshly ground black pepper
- ⅓ cup mixed herbs (chives, chervil, dill), chopped
  Salad greens

1. Wipe down the grate on your grill with a small amount of olive oil. Heat an electric grill to high or make a hot charcoal fire.

2. Season the salmon generously with salt and pepper. Drizzle with the olive oil and pat to rub in. Make a blanket of herbs on the filet.

3. Cook the filet skin side down on the grill with the cover closed for 5 minutes. Turn over and cook for an additional 5 minutes, or until just cooked through. With a long spatula, remove the fish from the grill and squeeze a little lemon juice over the filet.

4. For the dressing, whisk together the buttermilk, mayonnaise, sour cream, vinegar, garlic powder, onion powder, celery salt, Tabasco, salt, and pepper in a large bowl until well combined. Stir in the chopped herbs.

5. To serve, transfer the salmon to a large platter with a bowl of Buttermilk Dressing and a plate of your favorite salad greens on the side.

LAYERS OF FLAVOR: The poaching liquid, above, is scented with a bundle of fresh herbs tied with a string for easy retrieval. Local satsumas perfume the vinaigrette spooned atop the trout.

GINGER-POACHED TROUT WITH CITRUS VINAIGRETTE

Serves 6

Poaching is a wonderful way to prepare speckled trout, or any small trout such as rainbow or cutthroat. It's important that the filets are gently poached but never boiled. And remember to taste the poaching liquid to be sure your seasoning is perfect.

2 lemons, sliced

1 onion, sliced

1 bunch fresh thyme, tied

1 1-inch piece ginger, peeled and sliced

2 cloves garlic, sliced

Pinch red pepper flakes

1 bay leaf

Salt

Freshly ground black pepper

6 trout filets

FOR THE VINAIGRETTE

½ cup satsuma or orange juice

½ cup olive oil

Leaves from 1 sprig fresh basil, sliced

Salt

Freshly ground black pepper

2 cups baby greens

1. Fill a large heavy-bottomed pot with 2 inches of water. Add the lemons, onions, thyme, ginger, garlic, red pepper, and bay leaf. Bring to a gentle simmer and season with salt and pepper. Place the filets in the poaching broth and simmer for 6–8 minutes, until just cooked through. Remove the pot from the heat.

2. For the vinaigrette, whisk together the orange juice, olive oil, basil, salt, and pepper until well-incorporated.

3. In a bowl, toss the greens with the vinaigrette. To serve, carefully remove the filets from the poaching liquid, put a filet on each plate, and top with the salad greens.

WHOLE ROASTED SOLE WITH BROWN BUTTER

Serves 6

When I came through the ranks of chefdom, this dish could be found on the menu of every fancy French restaurant; the maitre d' would hold the dining room spellbound by deboning the sole with just a fork and a spoon. Whole roasted sole has lost its pretension but none of its cachet. Making it is much easier than you might think.

6	2-pound sole	1	cup (2 sticks) butter
2	cups flour		Juice of 1 lemon
	Salt	2	tablespoons capers
	Freshly ground black pepper	1	tablespoon chopped fresh parsley

1. Preheat the oven to 400°. Remove the skin from each fish by making a slit across the skin at the tail. Holding the fish in your hand with a towel, use needlenose pliers to pull the skin away from the sole. (This goes very fast!) Repeat on the other side. Salt the fish lightly.

2. Mix together the flour, salt, and pepper and spread on a plate. Dredge the fish in the flour mixture and shake off any excess.

3. Heat 2 tablespoons of the butter in a large skillet over medium high heat. Add the fish to the skillet one at a time, adding more butter as needed, and pan-fry, turning once, until golden brown. Transfer the sautéed fish to a roasting pan. Transfer to the oven and roast for 8–10 minutes, until just cooked through.

4. While the fish is roasting, make the brown butter sauce. Add the remaining butter to the skillet and cook over medium heat, stirring frequently to loosen the pan drippings and prevent clumps from forming. When the butter takes on a brown color, remove from the heat and add the lemon juice, capers, and parsley.

5. Remove the fish from the oven. For each fish, press a knife into the fin and press and pull to remove the fin. Repeat with the fin on the other side. With a fork and a knife, remove the backbone. Then remove the two filets from each side of the fish.

6. Serve the filets on a large platter with the brown butter sauce.

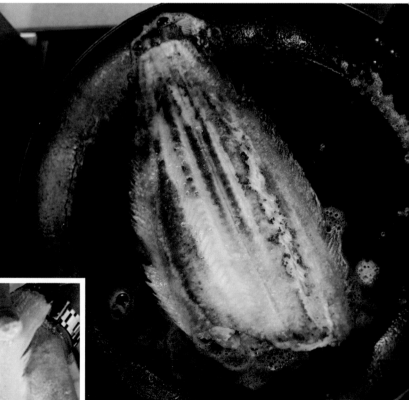

SOY-BRAISED SABLEFISH WITH COCONUT BROTH

Serves 6

You can use many other varieties of fish for this dish, but sablefish and black cod have the texture and oil content that work perfectly. Once seared, the fish filets gently stew in a fragrant coconut broth for just a few minutes before serving.

¼   cup soy sauce

3   tablespoons sugar

2   tablespoons tamari

2½ pounds skinned sablefish filets

¼   cup sesame oil

1   small onion, diced

2   cloves garlic, thinly sliced

1   1-inch piece ginger, peeled and sliced

1½ cups coconut milk
    Juice of 1 lime

1   tablespoon sambal chili paste

1   stalk lemongrass, split and bruised

1   cup chicken stock
    Leaves from 1 small bunch fresh basil, chopped
    Leaves from 1 small bunch fresh cilantro, chopped

1. In a large bowl, combine the soy sauce, sugar, and tamari. Toss the filets in the marinade and refrigerate for 1 hour.

2. In a large heavy-bottomed skillet, heat the sesame oil over high heat. Remove the fish from the marinade and shake off any excess. Sear the filets in the hot oil on both sides. Transfer the fish to a plate.

3. Add the onion, garlic, and ginger to the pan and stir over medium heat to soften. Add the coconut milk, lime juice, chili paste, and lemongrass. Cook for a minute, then add the chicken stock. Bring to a boil, cooking the sauce at a brisk simmer for about 10 minutes to reduce by half.

4. Return the filets to the pan with the sauce. Top with the cilantro and basil. Cover and simmer 5 more minutes before serving.

BAYOU BOATHOUSE: The charming structure, above, behind our house is a contemporary version of the old fishing shacks that line the waterways of Southern Louisiana. Making Potato Chip–Crusted Drum, right.

POTATO CHIP–CRUSTED DRUM WITH SAMBAL MAYONNAISE

Serves 6

This dish was inspired by my friend, chef Paul Kahan of Blackbird in Chicago, who uses walleye in his version. I came home and made it with black drum and red drum. I find it wildly delicious. Thanks Paul!

4 cups potato chips
2 cups Wondra flour
3 cups buttermilk
6 5-ounce drum filets
Salt
Olive oil for pan-frying

FOR THE SAMBAL MAYONNAISE

2 cups mayonnaise
3 piquillo peppers
3 tablespoons sambal chili paste
Juice of 1 lemon
Salt
Freshly ground black pepper

1. In a food processor, grind the potato chips and Wondra flour until they resemble coarse meal, then spread on a plate. Put the buttermilk in a shallow bowl. Season the fish with salt, then dip into the buttermilk. Shake off the excess, then dredge in the potato chip mixture.

2. In a heavy skillet, heat ¼ inch of olive oil over medium-high heat. Place the filets in the oil and pan-fry on both sides until golden brown.

3. For the mayonnaise, combine all the ingredients in a food processor or blender and mix well until incorporated. Season with salt and pepper. Serve the mayonnaise with the fish.

PAN-ROASTED GROUPER WITH SHELLFISH TOMATO SAUCE

Serves 6

All dense, meaty fish such as grouper, cobia, or mahimahi take especially well to pan-roasting. This is really easy: I sear the fish in the skillet and remove it quickly. Then, I use all of the juices and flavors in the pan as a base for a simple sauce. Here, I use the Shellfish Broth (page 26) I keep in the freezer. I freeze the stock in ice cube trays. Then I pop the cubes into a Ziploc bag and back into the freezer so I can use a couple to make a flavorful sauce anytime.

6 6-ounce skinless portions grouper

   Leaves from 2 sprigs fresh thyme, chopped

1 pinch crushed red pepper flakes

   Salt

   Freshly ground black pepper

¼ cup plus 2 tablespoons olive oil

1 clove garlic, minced

¼ cup Shellfish Broth (page 26)

¼ cup Cherry Tomato Five-Minute Sauce (page 26) or good tomato sauce

1. Season the filets with the thyme, red pepper, salt, and black pepper. Heat the ¼ cup olive oil in a large heavy skillet over medium-high heat. Add the fish and sear, frequently spooning the olive oil from the pan over the tops of the fish. Cook for 5–7 minutes on each side, until just cooked through. Transfer the fish to a serving platter and keep warm as you make the sauce.

2. Add the remaining 2 tablespoons olive oil and the garlic to the pan and stir with a wooden spoon to scrape up the good bits. After a minute, add the Shellfish Broth and tomato sauce. Season with salt and pepper. Bring to a boil, then reduce the heat and simmer for 5 minutes. To serve, spoon the sauce over the filets and enjoy.

SALT-BAKED STRIPED BASS
Serves 6

At first glance you might be afraid that the salt crust will make the fish itself taste intensely salty. But it doesn't. When you leave the skin and scales on the fish then pack it in the salt/egg white mixture to bake, the fish actually steams within its skin, yielding the most juicy and succulent flesh ever.

1 2–3-pound whole striped bass, scales and skin on	1 pound kosher salt
	¼ cup olive oil
	Juice of ½ lemon
1 bunch fresh thyme	1 clove garlic, thinly sliced
2 egg whites	

1. Preheat the oven to 350°. Stuff the cavity of the fish with the thyme branches. In a large bowl, beat the egg whites to medium peaks. Add the salt and mix until the texture is dry and crumbly. Line a baking sheet with foil and place the bass in the middle. Mound the salt mixture around the bass, patting it down like a snowball to completely cover the fish. Bake for 30–40 minutes, until the crust is golden.

2. Remove the fish from the oven and allow to cool slightly. Break the salt crust away from the fish. (This is easier than it sounds.) In a small saucepan, heat the olive oil, lemon juice, and garlic until warm. Carefully remove the skin of the fish and scoop a portion of bass onto each dinner plate. Drizzle the flavored oil over the bass and serve.

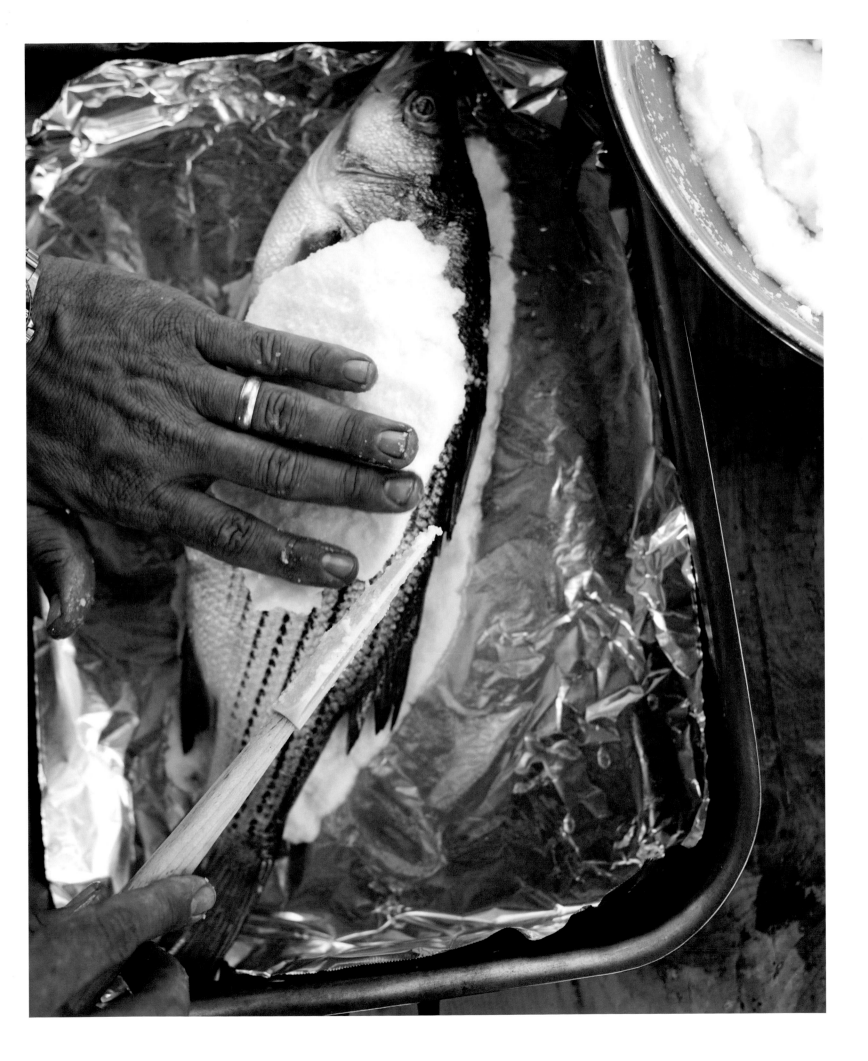

CRISPY SEARED SNAPPER WITH A LIGHT TOMATO SAUCE
Serves 6

Cooking fish well starts with an excellent fish-monger who you can rely on to scale, fillet, and cut to order your snapper (or other white, flaky fish like striped bass or redfish). We depend on my old friend Brian Cappy, of Kenney's in Slidell, Louisiana. He's a fish man you can trust. See Resources, page 254.

6	6-ounce skin-on snapper filets, scaled	1	teaspoon crushed red pepper flakes
	Olive oil	⅔	cup white wine
	Salt	½	cup cream
	Freshly ground black pepper	4	tablespoons butter
1	12-ounce can diced tomatoes	½	teaspoon pimentón
1	teaspoon minced garlic		Leaves from 1 sprig fresh thyme

1. Preheat the oven to 400°. With a sharp knife, score the fleshy side of each filet a few times.

2. Heat a large heavy skillet over medium-high heat, then coat the pan with a thin film of olive oil. Pat the filets dry with a paper towel and season with salt and pepper. Place the fish pieces in the pan skin side down and sear until the flesh begins to turn opaque, about 5 minutes.

3. Place the filets skin side up on a baking sheet and slide into the oven. Bake for 5 minutes, while you make the tomato sauce.

4. In the same skillet you cooked the fish, add the tomatoes, garlic, and red pepper flakes. Stir for a minute then pour in the white wine. Cook for another minute, stir in the cream, and let the liquid reduce by half. Add the butter, pimentón, and thyme. Season with salt and pepper. Remove the filets from the oven to individual plates and top with the sauce to serve.

FRIENDS INDEED are those who'll clean your fish for you! Drew Mire, left, and Patrick Berrigan in our boathouse.

"As a product of our little enclave of extreme South Louisiana…

I often felt that I wasn't exactly from the South. In fact our cooking at home had very little that truly resembled Deep South culture, including fried chicken. So many folks in and around New Orleans would look at that other South as if it were a completely different world, with strange accents. They'd compare our liberal drinking laws to their dry laws, our parishes to their counties; to many of us, they seemed like the mainstream America we saw on TV. I, on the other hand, had Deep South family and regularly floated between

these two distinct worlds—between the fried soft-shell crabs of coastal Louisiana and the fried chicken of my maternal grandparents' house in Alabama. My wife, Jenifer, would need me to translate on several of our early voyages to my grandmother's, even though it was just a couple of hours north of New Orleans.

Over the years, I spent school holidays and summer breaks working for and learning life lessons from my grandparents, Grace and Mitchell Walters. I traveled by train to visit them just as often as I could get away with it. Once I hit my teens, it was time for me to work every time I visited their furniture-making town. And work I did. I packed furniture, then delivered and unpacked it. I collected monthly payments from folks at their doors. This got me invited into most of the houses in town, where I'd be exposed to a vast array of hospitality and, of course, fried chicken. In that part of the South, the chicken would be washed down with a "cold drink," meaning an RC Cola. I loved it. Being away from my parents meant all the freedom a boy could want, and all the fried chicken he could eat.

My grandparents had a wonderful lady they employed called Miss Ruth, who was really part of the family. A wonderful part. She'd help Grandmother with Wednesday dinner, which was really lunch. The whole town would close at noon on Wednesdays, and that was extra special because Wednesday dinner meant fried chicken.

FRIED MEMORIES:
My son Luke tucks into a fried chicken drumstick just as I did as a boy, below. Right, chicken frying. Opposite from top, a tin chicken in Abita Springs, La., a fried lunch on the porch, and my niece, Jordan Bourgault.

When Grandmother fried it, the chicken had a uniformly breaded and flaky crust. Grandmother marinated her chicken in buttermilk then dredged it in flour seasoned with salt and pepper. She'd fry it in a cast iron pan with about an inch of peanut oil, cooking it with the lid on and flipping the pieces every so often, so that the color was uniformly golden brown. Her chicken was so crunchy, so juicy, and so missed today.

Miss Ruth's fried chicken couldn't have been more different. It had a battered crust that seemed just as thin as the chicken skin itself— perfectly crisp and light. She'd dip it in milk, then in seasoned flour. Miss Ruth would fry her chicken in a cast iron pan with more hot oil than Grandmother used. She wouldn't measure much or worry about temperatures, she just knew. She could tell when the oil was ready, because she'd float a match in it and wait for the match to ignite before she started cooking. Apparently, those white tip matches will light up at around 350°. (I don't recommend this method!) Once the chicken was done, she'd let it rest for a moment on some napkins out of the way, always afraid someone would burn themselves. But I'd manage to run off with a piece before anyone else got to taste. The crust would crack open and a sensuous steam would fill my nostrils before I could take a bite, the flesh pulling from the bone with delicious ease, all but melting in my mouth. Salt and pepper only made Miss Ruth's chicken taste better.

I'll forever debate the virtues of Grandmother's and Miss Ruth's recipes and will never decide on a winner. It was never a competition anyway, just each woman cooking from her heart. Since those days I've been hooked on fried chicken and since those days I've only had but twice chicken that equaled Miss Ruth's or my grandmother's. Both are in New Orleans.

Miss Willie Mae Seaton, who owned and operated Willie Mae's Scotch House in the Treme made chicken like Miss Ruth's. My friend, Kerry Seaton, Willie Mae's great-granddaughter, continues the tradition. My grandmother's fried chicken is closest to Leah Chase's at Dooky Chase, a restaurant just a block away from Willie Mae's. Dr. King, Nelson Mandela, President Kennedy, and other icons of the Civil Rights movement all dined with Miss Leah when they came to town. Today, when I'm frying up a batch of chicken, it's thoughts like these that run across my mind.

MY GRANDMOTHER'S FRIED CHICKEN
Serves 6

It's this classic buttermilk batter that gives chicken its crunchy texture. The batter should just barely adhere to the chicken, so make sure you give each piece a little shake to let extra batter drop off before frying. After the chicken is in the hot oil, my grandmother would put the lid on her pot and a kind of pressure cooker thing begins to happen inside, meaning the meat inside gets to cook, leaving the outside crispy.

1	free-range, organic chicken, cut into 8 pieces	1	quart buttermilk
	Salt	3	cups flour
	Freshly ground black pepper		Canola oil

1. Season the chicken pieces generously with salt and pepper. In a large bowl, soak the chicken in the buttermilk for at least 15 minutes. The idea is that the lactic acids tenderize the chicken. Sometimes my grandmother would even put the soaking chicken in the fridge overnight.

2. Mix the flour, salt, and pepper together and spread on a plate. Dredge each chicken piece in the seasoned flour to coat well.

3. Heat about 1 inch of canola oil in a cast iron pan until it reads 350° on a candy thermometer. In small batches, place a few pieces of the chicken in the oil at a time and fry for 6–8 minutes. Using a slotted spoon, turn each piece over, then cover the pan to cook for an additional 6 minutes. Drain on paper towels and salt well.

MISS RUTH'S FRIED CHICKEN
Serves 6

Miss Ruth used a wet batter, just seasoned flour and milk, which made her crust so thin and crispy. Although the cast iron pan retains heat well, it's important to add one piece of chicken to the pan every couple of minutes because each time you add a big chunk of chicken, the oil cools down. A good candy thermometer really helps here; it's even more crucial with this wet batter to maintain 350° throughout. Otherwise, you'll wind up with a mostly batter-y oil instead of crisp fried chicken. So cook in batches, no more than 4 pieces at a time.

1 free-range, organic chicken, cut into 8 pieces
Salt
Freshly ground black pepper
3 cups flour
1 tablespoon onion powder
1 tablespoon garlic powder
¼ teaspoon cayenne pepper
1 quart milk
Canola oil

1. Season the chicken pieces generously with salt and pepper. Mix the flour, the onion and garlic powders, the cayenne pepper, and ¼ teaspoon black pepper together and spread on a plate. Pour the milk into a bowl. Dip the chicken in the milk and then dredge through the seasoned flour to coat well.

2. Heat 3–4 inches of canola oil in a cast iron pan to 350° on a candy thermometer. (Miss Ruth liked to fry her chicken almost submerged in oil.) Drop the chicken, piece by piece, into the oil. (Do this in batches of 4 pieces.) Fry for 10–12 minutes, then turn the chicken over, cover the pan, and fry for an additional 8 minutes. Drain on paper towels and salt well.

PAN-FRIED PORK CHOPS
Serves 6

I happen to love pan-fried anything. Willie Mae Seaton's son Slim Charles Seaton, does the best fried pork chops at Willie Mae's. One day he revealed his secret: pork chops have a tendency to curl up as they cook, so he told me to make a small cut in the round end of the chop and it will curl no longer!

6	½-inch-thick pork rib chops	4	eggs, beaten
	Salt	1	cup milk
	Freshly ground black pepper	1½	cups flour
6	fresh sage leaves	½	cup finely grated Parmesan cheese
6	thin slices country ham or prosciutto		Olive oil or canola oil

1. Season the pork chops with salt and pepper. Press a sage leaf onto each chop and wrap the chop with a ham slice.

2. Set two shallow bowls in a row, one with the eggs mixed with the milk and one with the flour mixed with the Parmesan. Dip the chops into the eggy milk, then dredge in the flour and cheese mixture.

3. Heat ½ inch of oil in a cast iron pan over medium-high heat. Cook the pork chops, a few at a time, until each side is well-browned and cooked through, about 6 minutes a side. Drain on paper towels and salt well.

4. I love pork chops with Olive Oil–Roasted Cauliflower (page 48) and Cheesy Baked Polenta (page 52).

FRIED EGGPLANT SALAD
Serves 6

This dish allows me the thrill of eating fried eggplant without the guilt because it's a salad! I add bright greens, tomatoes, and crunchy peppers to a mild vinaigrette to lighten up the eggplant. It's important not to fry the eggplant until you're almost ready to serve the salad. But you can batter up the pieces in advance and keep them a short while in the refrigerator until you're ready. I don't recommend doing this ahead with almost any other dish, but it works well for eggplant.

2 eggs, beaten

1 cup bread crumbs

1 large eggplant, peeled and cut into 1- by 2-inch pieces

Olive oil

Salt

Freshly ground black pepper

¼ cup pecan oil or olive oil

2 tablespoons rice wine vinegar

3 handfuls mixed greens (small leaves)

1 cup thinly sliced red, green, and yellow bell peppers, or 1 cup Spanish Padrón peppers, dropped in the eggplant frying oil until blistered

1 cup cherry tomatoes, halved

Leaves from 3 sprigs fresh basil

Parmesan cheese, for shaving

1. Prepare two shallow bowls, one with the eggs and the other with the bread crumbs. Dip the eggplant pieces first into the eggs and then roll in the bread crumbs.

2. Heat about ½ inch of olive oil in a large cast iron pan over medium-high heat. In small batches, drop the battered eggplant pieces into the oil and fry until golden brown, about 5 minutes. Drain on paper towels and season with salt and pepper.

3. Mix up the pecan oil, vinegar, and salt in a bowl and toss with the greens, peppers, tomatoes, and basil leaves. Transfer to a serving platter and top with the fried eggplant. Use a vegetable peeler to shave a few shards of Parmesan over the salad.

PERFECT FRENCH FRIES

Serves 4

Perfect French fries must be fried twice, first blanched in hot oil to evaporate the water; then cooled and fried again so that they're crispy and cooked all the way through. The water and starch content of big, firm brown russet potatoes makes them an excellent choice for frying.

> 3 russet potatoes, peeled
> Canola oil
> Salt

1. Cut the potatoes into long sticks about ¼ inch thick.

2. To blanch the potatoes, heat 4 inches of oil in a heavy-bottomed pot to 300° on a candy thermometer. In small batches, drop the potatoes in the oil and cook for 5–6 minutes. The potatoes should wilt but not take on color.

3. Remove the potatoes from the oil with a slotted spoon and drain on paper towels. Don't discard the oil. This can be done in advance and the potatoes kept in the refrigerator for a couple of hours.

4. Just before serving, raise the temperature of the oil to 350° and refry the potatoes in batches until they've turned a lovely golden brown. Drain on paper towels and salt well.

PAN-FRIED TURKEY SCHNITZEL

Serves 6

While a schnitzel is traditionally made with veal, turkey is much less expensive and, oddly enough, it's easier to find good turkey than good veal. In fact, now you can buy good organic turkey in the supermarket. I sometimes fry the slices in advance for Jenifer to reheat later in the week. You can pound them thinner if you wish, or just slice the breast ¼ inch thick.

I like to use Japanese panko bread crumbs, which are lighter and airier than regular bread crumbs. What I do differently is to pulse them a few times in the food processor so I get superfine bread crumbs like those I used to find in Southern Germany where I learned my schnitzel moves.

> 1 3-pound turkey breast
> Salt
> Freshly ground black pepper
> 4 eggs, beaten
> 1 cup milk
>
> 2 cups flour
> 2 cups panko bread crumbs, pulsed in a food processor
> Olive oil or canola oil

1. Slice the turkey breast into ¼-inch-thick cutlets. Season well with salt and pepper.

2. Set three shallow bowls in a row, one with the beaten eggs mixed with the milk, one with the flour, and one with the panko. Dip the turkey cutlets first in the eggy milk, then dredge in the flour, then press into the panko, making sure to coat the slices well.

3. Heat about ½ inch of canola oil in a cast iron pan over medium-high heat. Carefully slide the turkey cutlets into the oil a few at a time. Brown each cutlet on both sides for 5–7 minutes a side. Drain on paper towels and salt well.

4. Serve with noodles or add slices of cheese for an instant turkey Parmigiana. Squeeze a bit of lemon over the top if you like.

FRIED CATFISH

Serves 6

Imported fish give catfish a bad rap! I have a friend at the Crescent City Farmers Market in New Orleans who sells wild-caught catfish from the lakes near Des Allemands, Louisiana. The fish is night and day better than any of that dubious stuff imported from Asia that is too often passed off as catfish. Find a fishmonger you trust to get you good, honest catfish.

6 catfish filets, boneless and skinless
Salt
Freshly ground black pepper

2 eggs, beaten
1 cup milk
3 cups fine-ground cornmeal
Canola oil

1. Generously season the filets with salt and pepper. Set out two shallow bowls. Mix the beaten eggs with the milk in one bowl and put the cornmeal in the other. Dip the filets first in the eggy milk, then dredge in the cornmeal.

2. Heat 3 inches of canola oil in a heavy-bottomed skillet over medium-high heat to 350° on a candy thermometer. In batches, gently slide the filets into the oil and fry for 6 minutes. Turn the pieces over with a slotted spoon and cook an additional 4 minutes. Drain on paper towels and season well.

Barbecue Wisdom

"Few meals are as memorable to me as the great barbecues in my life…

Yet it's funny how the word barbecue, with all its connotations, engenders so much passion, misinformation, and downright lack of tolerance. I've seen otherwise pretty open-minded men display real anger when the subject turns to the best ways to barbecue. Truth is, we have so many preconceived notions about "real" barbecue that if you come from a barbecue state, you're probably already too biased for civil discussion.

One of my more frustrating times was as a young cook in Europe. Although I consider that experience my culinary awakening, one thing that truly rankled was the way poorly grilled anything was referred to as "American," or worse, "BBQ." I can't tell you how often I'd have to bite my tongue, as I could hardly inform accomplished master chefs that barbecue was way more my area of expertise than theirs. What they did wasn't barbecue, it was overcooked food on a grill. Restaurants were never the setting for bad barbecue; it would happen at casual events, like a staff appreciation picnic, where a paltry fire would be lit in some cheap grill. The burned result was nothing like my memories from home. As a representative of Southern Americans, I tried to be polite, with a quick "Oui, Chef" or "Jawohl, Chef," but deep down, fierce opinions I did have: Abuse of barbecue being, of course, a criminal offense.

(Here I must admit that in New Orleans we love our barbecued shrimp, which has absolutely nothing to do with a grill or a smoker, but is so tasty: shrimp sautéed in a big pan with lots of ground black pepper and butter, its flavor enhanced by the heads and shells of the shrimp. And of course chunks of French bread to sop up the sauce. But I digress.) Getting back to my many European barbecue experiences, if you're ever invited to one, just say "Non, merci" and run.

SCENES FROM A BARBECUE: From left, a buffet lunch with some of my favorite dishes; corn in the husk ready for the grill; the dogs salivate. Opposite, Little LeRoy, the smoker, doing its job; the cochon de lait is ready to eat.

It wasn't until I married Jenifer that I got to know barbecue in an intimate way: we ate it every day on our honeymoon in the mountains of western North Carolina. At the Carolina Smokehouse in Cashiers, I tasted the best pulled pork and ribs I'd ever had. Ever since, I've tried to travel and eat barbecue, from the Low Country of the Carolinas, to Kansas City, to the Gulf Coast of Alabama, to the Mississippi Delta and Memphis, savoring every little delectable tidbit along the way, learning bite by bite the source of authentic flavor.

It took Texas Hill Country barbecue to convert me into a passionate aficionado of barbecued beef, in particular brisket and beef ribs. I'm not sure if it was Cooper's Old Time Pit Bar-B-Que in Llano or Smitty's Market or Kreuz Market in Lockhart that enlightened me, but it damn sure happened in Texas. The epiphany more than likely occurred when I saw their large pits that echoed our South Louisiana make-shift "Cajun Microwave"—our method of barbecuing cochon de lait (page 168).

The ingredients surely differ, as do the wood and the type of pit, but when it comes down to it, barbecue is really all about seasoning the meat properly and cooking it either quickly on the grill, or covered, low and slow, over indirect heat (which has a similar effect on meat as braising does, the moist heat slowly tenderizing a tough but flavorful cut). And that's about all a boy from the bayou would ever know about barbecue.

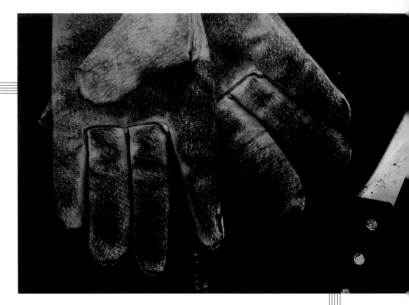

Notes on Grilling

I SEEM TO HAVE A GRILL for every occasion around my house. Truth be told, grilling outside is our favorite way to cook at home. It's easy and less messy. That's right—I'm lazy and grilling is for sure the lazy man's way to cook. For my wife, there is no faster way for her to cook for the boys than to fire up the propane grill and make dinner outdoors while the lads play ball in the backyard.

Grills come in every shape and size these days and if used properly they're all pretty effective. But not all foods should be grilled in the same manner. I love the flavor wood—and a charcoal-fired grill—imparts to some foods; but sometimes too much smoke is too much. In wood and charcoal grilling, what really matters is to make sure to heat the grill so the grate gets really hot and ensures that the food doesn't stick. The other technique I can share is to arrange the coals on your grill so that you have one really hot side and one less-hot side. That way you can hot-sear food then move it to the cooler side or the grill, allowing it ample time to cook through. Use the same technique for a propane grill: allow time to let the grates preheat before using.

I find that grilled and smoked foods—especially meats—do better if they're slightly cured before grilling. This means using a dry rub the night before or briefly curing the meat in a wet brine an hour or so before you grill. This works because the brine or dry rub has a curing effect on the proteins on the surface, which gives the meat a juicier mouth feel and allows the meat to better absorb the smoky flavors of the grill. I always put a bit of sugar in my brines and dry rubs to help the meat caramelize on the outside, deepening and sweetening the flavor.

There's just no substitute for a smoker. It cooks things long and slow at temperatures of 300° or less for hours with no worry. My big old smoker on wheels, Little LeRoy (yes it does have a name and yes it is a long story which I'll spare you), is a commitment. To smoke on Little LeRoy means doing a good bit of work, like building the fire, keeping it well lit, and using a series of dampers to control airflow and heat retention, just like the thermostat on your kitchen oven. The key to successful smoking is proper prep time: making sure to cure the meats or fish well ahead and to construct the fire long before cooking begins. And of course there's the cochon de lait, smoked suckling pig, for which we use the Cajun Microwave (page 168).

DRY-RUBBED PORK RIBS

Serves 6

Just the sight of whole racks of baby back pork ribs smoking away on Little LeRoy is enough to make me feel that all is right with the world.

3 racks baby back ribs
½ cup Pork & Chicken Dry
    Rub (recipe right)

1. The night before, generously season the ribs with the Dry Rub on all sides. Cover and refrigerate overnight.

2. Preheat the smoker to 325°. Place the rib racks in the smoker, bone side down. Smoke for 5 hours, or until they turn mahogany brown. My trick for telling when the meat is done: when it can be pulled away from the bone with a grilling fork with relative ease.

PORK & CHICKEN DRY RUB

Makes about 3¾ cups

Surely this dry rub can be used with just about any meat, but I particularly favor Dry-Rubbed Smoked Chicken (page 160). Mix it up ahead of time and keep it in a jar in the pantry.

2 cups sugar
1 cup salt
1 tablespoon Chinese
   five-spice powder

1 teaspoon cayenne
   pepper

1. Mix the ingredients together and store in a Mason jar. Rub into the meat well, preferrably the night (or at least a few good hours) before you plan to barbecue.

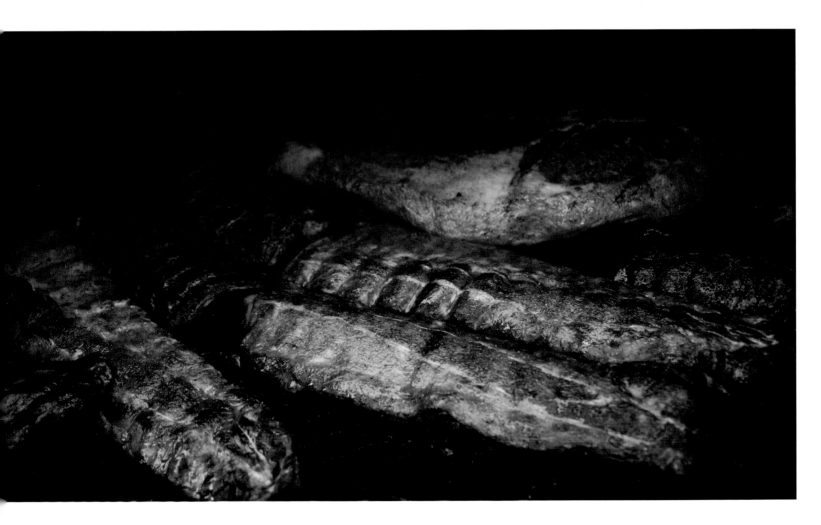

TENDER SLOW-COOKED BEEF BRISKET

Serves 10

Barbecued brisket is, in reality, smoked. Doing it properly is an art, especially in the South. Here I let the brisket pick up its wonderful smoky flavor outside, then wrap it well and finish it indoors in a low oven so it's falling-apart tender.

1   5–6-pound beef brisket
½   cup Beef Dry Rub
    (recipe right)

1. The night before, generously season the brisket with the Dry Rub on all sides. Wrap well in plastic wrap and refrigerate overnight.

2. Preheat the smoker to 250°. Lay the brisket in the smoker and smoke for 6 hours, adding wood as needed along the way to maintain a near-perfect 250°. It's important to remember to adjust the dampers to regulate heat. When the brisket is tender, remove it from the smoker, wrap it in foil, and place in a 200° oven for an additional 2 hours to continue the slow cooking process toward perfection. To serve, trim away the excess fat (which I like to add to my Baked Beans, page 161, for more flavor) and slice against the grain.

BEEF DRY RUB

Makes about 3½ cups

This rub is quite classic but it works well, too, as a brine for meat and poultry when diluted with enough water to cover—so you've got the perfect combination of salty/sweet. Or, use the dry base as a wet rub, adding just enough olive oil to form a paste. It's wonderful slathered on a whole leg of lamb.

1   cup brown sugar
1   cup kosher salt
1   tablespoon freshly ground black pepper
1   tablespoon pimentón

1   tablespoon garlic powder
1   tablespoon onion powder
¼   teaspoon cayenne pepper

1. Mix the ingredients together and store in a Mason jar. Rub into the meat well, preferably the night before.

GRILLED CORN ON THE COB

Serves 6

Grilling corn in the husk actually steams the corn and gives it a smoky flavor. When you remove the husk, the kernels are tender and sweet. Don't worry if the husks burn, the corn will just taste better.

6   ears of corn in their husks, silks removed

Softened butter

1. In a large bowl or pail of warm water that tastes as salty as the sea, soak the corn in their husks for 2 hours.

2. Preheat a gas or charcoal grill to medium. Place the corn on the grill and cook for 30 minutes, turning often. The outer leaves will burn, which is just fine. Remove the corn from the heat. When cool enough to handle, pull back the husks from the corn and tie back to serve. Butter the ears while the corn is still hot.

ROASTED RED PEPPER SALAD

Serves 6

This is a great salad to make even without a grill. Just turn the oven on 500° and put the peppers right on the oven rack for 5–7 minutes, until their skins blister. Proceed with the rest of the recipe. However, if I'm firing up the grill anyway, I'll throw the peppers on along with a mixture of raw vegetables that Jenifer can use for the boys' dinners throughout the week. This salad can be made a day or two in advance.

6–8 red bell peppers
4 tablespoons olive oil
½ red onion, thinly sliced
1 tablespoon red wine vinegar
Leaves from 1 sprig fresh thyme
1 pinch pimentón
Salt
Freshly ground black pepper

1. Preheat a gas or charcoal grill to high. Rub the peppers all over with 1 tablespoon of the olive oil and place on the grill using tongs. Grill until slightly charred and blistered on all sides. Transfer to a Ziploc bag and refrigerate until cool.

2. Once cool, use a paring knife to scrape and remove the skins and seeds under cool running water. When they're peeled, quarter the peppers.

3. Place the peppers and onions in a bowl and toss with the remaining 3 tablespoons olive oil, the vinegar, thyme, and pimentón. Taste and season well with salt and pepper. Let sit 30 minutes before serving.

ALON'S PIZZA ON THE GRILL
Makes 6

Alon Shaya is the chef at Domenica, our Italian restaurant in New Orleans. He studied the art of Italian cooking and advises: "The easiest way to do pizza on a standard propane-fueled grill is to heat one side of the grill to high and set the other side to medium. You want to cook the crust quickly on high heat, yet inevitably it won't fully cook in the center before the crust begins to char in places. So I like to grill each side for a good 15 seconds or so on high, then move it to the cooler side of the grill.

Then I'll lay on the sauce, cheese, and toppings and put the cover on so the cheese can melt. Or slide the pizza from the hot grill onto a baking sheet and into a hot oven to finish cooking."

3½	cups bread flour, plus more as needed	1	tablespoon active dry yeast
4½	teaspoons kosher salt	3	tablespoons olive oil
1½	cups lukewarm water (95°–100°)		Sauce, cheese, and toppings of your choice
1	tablespoon sugar		

1. Combine the flour and salt in a small bowl. Mix the the warm water and sugar in the bowl of a standing mixer fitted with a dough hook. Sprinkle the yeast over the water and let stand until the yeast begins to foam. This should take about 10 minutes.

2. Add the olive oil to the yeast mixture and mix until blended. Add the flour mixture and mix until a soft, very sticky dough forms. Continue to add flour, a tablespoon at a time, until the dough is smooth and does not stick to the side of the mixing bowl.

3. Lightly coat the inside of a separate bowl with a bit more olive oil. Place the dough in the oiled bowl and brush lightly with olive oil. Cover the bowl with a damp kitchen towel and let the dough rise in a warm area of the kitchen until doubled in volume, about 1 hour.

4. Preheat one side of a gas grill to high and the other to medium. If using a charcoal grill, burn coals until completely white, then arrange them so that you have a hot side and a cooler side.

5. Turn the dough out onto a work surface with no flour. Divide into 6 pieces, each about the size of a tennis ball. Roll each piece into a ball. Put the dough balls on a baking sheet, cover with plastic wrap, and let rest in a warm place for 15 minutes.

6. Use a rolling pin to roll out each ball on a floured surface until it is about 8 inches in diameter. With a long spatula or a pizza peel (or your fingers), carefully place a dough round onto the hot side of the grill and cook, turning once, until grill marks are visible, about 15 seconds on each side. Remove from the grill and add desired toppings. Return pizza to the cooler side of the grill and cover or put on a baking sheet and into a 450° oven; cook until the cheese is melted. Repeat with the remaining dough balls.

CLASSIC MARGHERITA GRILLED PIZZA
Makes 1

A tomato, mozzarella, and basil pizza is traditional, but you can also get creative and top the grilled pizza crusts with whatever ingredients you like.

1	grilled pizza crust (above)	¼	cup diced fresh mozzarella cheese
¼	cup good tomato sauce		Leaves from 1 sprig fresh basil, torn

1. Spread the tomato sauce out evenly on the grilled pizza crust. Top with the mozzarella and basil leaves. Return to the grill or place in a 450° oven until the cheese is melted.

COCHON DE LAIT

Serves 10

As a child in South Louisiana, the only real barbecue I knew was our famed cochon de lait, or suckling pig, which refers to the young pig itself, along with the act of roasting the pig, as well as the delicious celebration that follows. Though I give instructions about cooking the pig in a Cajun Microwave (page 168), I presume most folks will use a large smoker and indirect heat, removing the cover for the last hour to let the skin crisp properly.

1 20-pound suckling pig, butterflied (ask your butcher to do this)	Pepper Jelly Barbecue Sauce (page 172)
1½ cups Cochon de Lait Dry Rub (recipe right)	

1. The night before, generously season the pig with the Dry Rub on all sides. Wrap in plastic and refrigerate.

2. Preheat the smoker to 250°. Lay the pig in the smoker and let smoke for 6 hours, flipping it every 1½ hours, until it turns a gorgeous mahogany brown. Add fuel as needed to the smoker box to maintain temperature. After 6 hours, remove the cover and cook for 1 more hour to crisp the skin. The cochon is ready once the skin is crisp and the meat is easily pulled from the bone with a fork.

3. To serve, distribute small plates or just mound the tender pork on a large platter and let everyone dig in, with the barbecue sauce served on the side for dipping.

COCHON DE LAIT DRY RUB

Makes about 1¾ cups

We've always used this rub on our suckling pigs, but it works well on a pork shoulder, or for that matter, anything porky.

1 cup kosher salt	1 teaspoon freshly ground black pepper
½ cup brown sugar	1 teaspoon pimentón
1 tablespoon garlic powder	½ teaspoon cayenne pepper
1 teaspoon onion powder	
1 teaspoon cumin	

1. Mix the ingredients together and store in a Mason jar.

PEPPER JELLY BARBECUE SAUCE

Makes about 2½ cups

As the base for this barbecue sauce, I love to use pepper jelly or sweet mayhaw preserves (or other good fruit preserves) mixed with grainy Creole mustard and vinegar cooked down with caramelized onions and tomato paste. I don't slather on the sauce or baste it over the pig. I prefer it as a dipping sauce on the side. Resources, page 254.

1 tablespoon canola oil	½ cup rice wine vinegar
1 onion, minced	2 tablespoons Creole mustard
2 cloves garlic, thinly sliced	Salt
2 tablespoons tomato paste	Freshly ground black pepper
1 10-ounce jar Tabasco pepper jelly	

1. Heat the oil in a small saucepan over medium-high heat. Add the onions and cook until caramelized and browned. Add the garlic and tomato paste. Stir and cook for 2 more minutes. Stir in the pepper jelly and vinegar. Continue to cook and stir until the jelly is dissolved. Cook for an additional 5 minutes, then add the Creole mustard. Reduce the heat to medium low and simmer for 20 minutes. Season with salt and pepper.

BARBECUE SAUCE

Serves 6

This basic sauce works well with any fruit jam. Instead of blackberry, I'll often use our local fig preserves. The key is to balance the sweetness of the fruit with vinegar and mustard.

1 tablespoon canola oil	2 heaping tablespoons Creole mustard
1 onion, chopped	1 clove garlic, minced
1½ cups blackberry or other fruit preserves	½ teaspoon cayenne pepper
¾ cup apple cider vinegar	
⅔ cup ketchup	

1. Heat the oil in a small saucepan over high heat. Add the onions and stir until golden brown. Lower the heat to medium and add the preserves, vinegar, ketchup, mustard, garlic, and cayenne, stirring well to incorporate. Reduce to a simmer and cook for 10 minutes. Remove from heat and allow to cool.

GRILLED AVOCADO & TOMATO SALAD

Serves 8

There is a common theme with my home cooking: I call it Kitchen Focus in Chapter 1, but what it's really about is planning. So many dishes can be done ahead of time and taste better for it. This salad, however, is not one of those make-ahead recipes. It must be done at the last possible minute and served immediately. A grill makes a delicious avocado even better. But a ripe avocado is so delicate it takes little cooking: just touch it to the grill for a moment to bring out its floral aroma.

1. Preheat a gas or charcoal grill to medium heat. Season the avocados with salt and pepper and rub with the olive oil and lime juice. Place the avocados flesh side down on the grill and cook for 5 minutes.

2. Arrange the tomato slices on a serving platter and generously season with salt and pepper. With a large soup spoon, remove the avocado halves from their skins and slice about ½ inch thick. Alternate the avocados with the tomatoes on the platter.

3. For the dressing, whisk together all of the ingredients, season with salt and pepper, and drizzle over the salad.

4 unpeeled avocados, halved, pits removed
Salt
Freshly ground black pepper
1 tablespoon olive oil
Juice of 1 lime
4 heirloom tomatoes, thinly sliced

FOR THE DRESSING
½ cup olive oil
2 tablespoons sherry vinegar
1 tablespoon avocado oil (optional)
Leaves from 2 sprigs fresh basil, minced
1 clove garlic, minced
½ teaspoon pimentón
Salt
Freshly ground black pepper

MY FAVORITE POTATO SALAD

Serves 8–10

Sometimes great marriages are made in the kitchen. Such was the case with this creamy potato salad when we introduced my egg salad to Jenifer's potato salad. A match made in heaven!

5–7	Yukon Gold potatoes, about 3 pounds	1	white onion, minced
8	large eggs	1	stalk celery, minced
		3	green onions, chopped
		1	clove garlic, minced

FOR THE DRESSING

1¼ cups mayonnaise

¼ cup rice wine vinegar

¼ cup sweet pickle relish

2 tablespoons Creole mustard

Salt

Freshly ground black pepper

1. Put the potatoes in a large heavy-bottomed pot and add salted water to cover by 2 inches. Bring to a boil, then reduce to a simmer and cook until the potatoes are fork tender, about 30 minutes. Drain and cool. When the potatoes are cool enough to handle, use a paring knife to remove the skin. Roughly chop the potatoes into bite-size pieces.

2. While the potatoes are cooking, place the eggs in a saucepan and cover with water. Bring the water to a boil over high heat, cover, and immediately remove from the heat. Let the eggs sit in the hot water for 5–7 minutes, then remove the lid and place the pot in the sink under the cold water faucet. Let the water run until the eggs have cooled enough to handle. Peel and roughly chop the eggs.

3. For the dressing, whisk together the mayonnaise, vinegar, relish, and mustard in a medium bowl until well combined. Add the onions, celery, green onions, and garlic and stir well.

4. Combine the potatoes and eggs in a large serving bowl. Add the dressing and stir to combine. Season with salt and pepper and refrigerate until ready to serve.

COLESLAW

Serves 6

We usually make coleslaw with whatever is in our pantry and refrigerator—the variations are endless and delicious. This version is tangy and sweet, which makes it a perfect complement to barbecue.

1	head cabbage, halved, cored, and thinly sliced	½	cup shredded carrots
2	onions, thinly sliced	1	cup mayonnaise
2	green onions, thinly sliced	1	cup rice wine vinegar
1	cup chopped sweet gherkin pickles	½	cup sugar

1. In a large serving bowl, mix together the cabbage, onions, green onions, gherkins, and carrots. In another bowl, whisk together the mayonnaise, vinegar, and sugar until well incorporated. Pour the dressing over the cabbage mixture and toss to coat well. Cover and refrigerate for an hour or so before serving.

BLACK-EYED PEA SALAD
Serves 8

This is one of those dishes that improves as it sits in the refrigerator. So feel free to make the peas and assemble the salad a day or two ahead of time. I substitute whatever field pea or legume I have on hand—lady creamer, purple hull, etc. I love that each variety makes the salad taste a little different, but it is always so good. Especially with barbecue.

1 pound black-eyed peas, cooked and drained (see Field Peas, page 55)

1 red onion, thinly sliced

2 tablespoons chopped chives

¾ cup canola oil or pecan oil

¼ cup pepper jelly

¼ cup rice wine vinegar

Salt

Freshly ground black pepper

1. Mix together the black-eyed peas, onions, and chives in a large serving bowl.

2. Whisk together the oil, pepper jelly, and vinegar in a small bowl until well combined. Pour over the black-eyed peas and toss the salad so that it is evenly dressed. Taste and season with salt and pepper.

chapter nine

Jazz Brunch

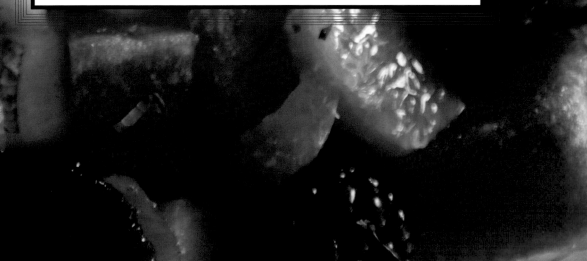

"Jazz Brunch: just saying the words is enough to put a smile on my face…

I've traveled a great deal of the world over, preaching the gospel of New Orleans culture. This often happens at a Jazz Brunch, where I'm paired with musicians like Allen Toussaint, Wynton Marsalis, Ronnie Kole, or local jazz artists in places likd the South of France. So much more than just another meal, Jazz Brunch is a celebration of our passion for food and music and can happen at a funeral or a wedding. Any day is a great excuse for this celebration of life

that combines artful elements of entertaining—music, food, dance, and even design—with a result that's joyous and fun. I come from people who have serious pride in their Southern hospitality, but I've never seen the gracious art of welcome taken to such heights as in France, where they seem to understand instinctively the meaning of effortless entertaining. My French "families," the Baurs and Bérauds, make hospitality a competitive sport, in which each host easily maintains his never-flustered cool.

Many years ago, I just dropped in on Jean Pierre Béraud at Le Rivage in Olivet, along the Loiret, a small sleepy tributary of the larger, busier Loire. I was traveling with my wife, Jenifer, and our then two-week-old baby, Brendan. Okay, I wasn't totally unexpected; Jean Pierre did have an idea I was coming, but had no idea when. Nor did any of us imagine we'd end up spending a week there. Moments after our unexpected arrival, we were shown to a table on the terrace under the magnificent ancient chestnut trees that line the bank of the Loiret and provide the perfect shade.

Before we got beyond niceties and introductions, glasses of Krug blanc de noir were in our hands; warm gougères suddenly appeared, literally exploding with Emmentaler at each bite. Jen, who was breast feeding at the time, was reassured that Champagne would be healthier for her than white wine. And, if she had any qualms about Champagne, she shouldn't worry, because their

OUR JAZZ BRUNCH:
The secret is to make plenty of food, and prepare it well ahead. From left, at the buffet, my son Luke, Jenifer, Claire Berrigan, and Dionne Strickland; showing Jimmy Strickland my iPhone; happy guests, Octavia Strickland with Molly and Erin Berrigan; Crab-Stuffed Avocados; and Jimmy Strickland III, enjoying himself.

ample supply of rouge would surely benefit both mother and child. The small talk led to a three-hour lunch of such local delectables as pâté de canard sauvage, entrecôte of Limousin beef, brochette of pike from the river, and crawfish in a creamy nage with sweet tarragon. For dessert there were William pears with crème fraîche and local honey.

As we ate, I was moved at how unrushed and nonchalant Jean Pierre seemed about this spur-of-the-moment lunch for his three young American friends. He chatted easily about what we'd have for dinner that night, and where we had to go for a picnic the next day. He introduced us to every soul who passed by, all of whom seemed genuinely happy to meet us and with heartfelt enthusiasm picked up Brendan and kissed his little head—remarking on his considerable girth and happy demeanor.

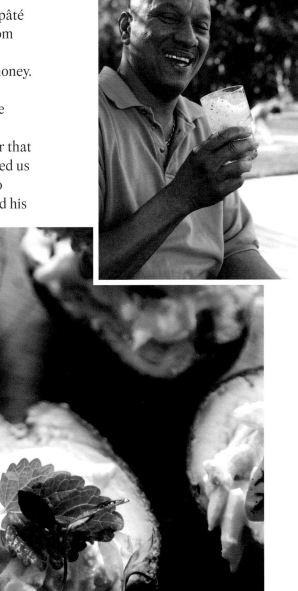

Jean Pierre's generous nature exemplifies graciousness and humility and he has left a profound impression on me. I learned that true hospitality lives in the heart of the host, not in a lavish spread of gourmet foods. When we throw a Jazz Brunch at home, I have Jean Pierre in my head as I welcome friends and family who arrive at our house, whether I expect them or not.

Entertaining Thoughts

I LIKE TO THROW A JAZZ BRUNCH for family birthdays and weddings. And since Sunday is the only day that works with nearly everyone's schedule, it's a natural Jazz Brunch day. Besides good people, to throw a Jazz Brunch you need good music, good drinks, and good food. The food part is easy. I love to create menus that are equal parts hot and cold, sweet and savory. My Jazz Brunch is always a buffet, which needn't mean boring. Make it as simple or as grand as you wish. The idea, of course, is to prepare almost everything ahead of time. Planning is key.

Put together a signature playlist of your favorite jazz. Vary the mix of music so your guests will stop and take notice. Keep it fun and lighthearted. Jazz is so much more than Dixieland, but even if you only have "Down by the Riverside," by all means play it. Loud. Anything to get feet tapping, hips wiggling, and people feeling like they wouldn't rather be anywhere else!

Drinks are important and nothing screams "brunch drink!" more than the gin-based Pimm's Cup, a New Orleans favorite that looks great in a big glass: all that fresh fruit with slightly sweet, slightly bitter undertones and a crispy slice of cucumber. And Champagne, of course, either straight and sparkly, or with a touch of fresh-squeezed satsuma juice and a splash of arancello liqueur. For the kids, set up a Smoothie Bar with a blender, bucket of ice, and pitchers of fruit juices, along with yogurt and fresh berries, chopped bananas, pineapple, and mango so they can create their own drinks, and a welcome bit of chaos in the process.

While you're serving drinks, have a few cold or room-temperature dishes ready for your guests to indulge in. Buffets needn't be the dreaded row of chafing dishes that sit there for hours. You've got great music and a lot of energy, so keep it moving by directing the flow to a table laden with delicious dishes you were so smart to have made in advance. I want folks to start nibbling upon arrival, so I lay out dishes taken right from the fridge just as the brunch begins; such delights as Pickled Shrimp, Marinated Crab Fingers, and Crab-Stuffed Avocados.

If it's a warm day, I'll ladle up chilled soups like Yellow Tomato Gazpacho. Because brunch is part breakfast, I love to serve the most delicious thing: a platter of crab cakes, each topped with a poached egg and a spoonful of satsuma hollandaise. Sometimes I do get a little flashy with a main course like Crown Roast of Pork, but what a looker on a buffet table! To wrap it up, think fresh fruits in season cut into a salad. And scour Chapter 11 for custards, cream pies, and cakes—anything that can be prepared a day or two in advance.

GROANING BOARD: Left, my three nieces Claire Berrigan, her sister Madeleine, and Kaitlyn Bourgault get first dibs before the throngs arrive.

PICKLED SHRIMP

Serves 10

This recipe requires high-quality wild shrimp. Of course, I prefer wild Louisiana shrimp from the waters I know. It's better to find the best shrimp than to worry about whether they've been frozen or not. Unless the shrimp come straight from the net to your kitchen, sometimes the highest quality are frozen. This is where a trusty fishmonger makes all the difference; see Resources, page 254.

You can mix up your vegetables with the shrimp, using whatever's fresh and local. I love to add cauliflower, carrots, daikon, beans, onions, mirliton, and/or okra.

FOR THE BRINE
- 2 cups rice wine vinegar
- Zest and juice of 1 lemon
- Zest and juice of 1 orange
- ½ cup sugar
- 5 cloves garlic, thinly sliced
- 1 tablespoon coriander seed
- 1 tablespoon mustard seed
- 1 tablespoon peppercorns
- 1 tablespoon red chili flakes
- 2 bay leaves
- Pinch kosher salt

FOR THE SHRIMP
- 12 baby carrots, peeled
- 12 green beans
- 12 pearl onions, peeled
- 12 okra pods
- 2 pounds boiled wild Louisiana shrimp, peeled and deveined

1. For the brine, combine all the ingredients in a large saucepan. Add 2½ cups water and bring to a boil. Remove from the heat and allow to cool slightly.

2. Pack all the vegetables and shrimp into a very large glass jar, alternating layers. Pour the hot brine into the jar to cover. Cover the jar and let cool. Refrigerate overnight. Serve right from the jar when you're ready.

BABE IN ARMS: Molly Berrigan is the apple of her grandmothers' eyes, Barbara Berrigan, left, and Marcia Mahoney.

YELLOW TOMATO GAZPACHO

Serves 8

Beautiful ripe yellow tomatoes make this golden tomato soup so gorgeous. You can use whatever tomatoes you can find as long as they're fresh and local. I look for heirloom tomatoes that are thin-skinned and sweet as can be.

- 1 tablespoon olive oil
- ½ white onion, diced
- 2 cloves garlic, sliced
- 2 pounds yellow tomatoes, cored and roughly chopped
- ½ cup diced stale bread
- 2 pinches pimentón
- 1 pinch sugar
- Salt
- Freshly ground black pepper
- Leaves from 1 small bunch fresh cilantro, chopped

1. Heat the oil in a heavy skillet over medium heat. Add the onions and garlic and sweat until soft, about 3 minutes. Add the tomatoes and cook for 5 minutes, breaking up the pieces with the back of a wooden spoon. Add the bread and pimentón and mix well. Add the sugar and salt and pepper to taste. Remove from the heat.

2. Sprinkle the cilantro over the tomato mixture. Use a food mill or a food processor to purée the soup in batches. Transfer to a bowl and refrigerate. Serve chilled in cups or small glasses.

DEVILED EGGS WITH TENNESSEE TRUFFLES

Serves 8

Dr. Tom Michaels is a scientist and a pioneer in raising American black truffles, cultivated under chestnut trees in Tennessee. Truffles may be expensive, but I think they're worth it to really elevate this humble dish. (See Resources, page 254.) Here's an egg trick I learned from Chef Erick Loos at La Provence: coat the eggs with a little olive oil before boiling to make them easier to peel!

8	eggs	1	teaspoon Dijon mustard
½	cup mayonnaise		Salt
¼	white onion, minced		Freshly ground black pepper
2	tablespoons rice wine vinegar	1	tablespoon minced black truffle
2	tablespoons olive oil		

1. For perfect hard-boiled eggs, place the eggs in a saucepan and cover with water. Bring the water to a boil over high heat, cover, and immediately remove from heat. Let the eggs sit in the hot water for 5–7 minutes, then remove the lid and place the pot in the sink under cold running water. Let the water run until the eggs have cooled enough to handle.

2. Peel the eggs and slice in half. Remove the yolks to a large bowl and whisk with the mayonnaise, onions, vinegar, olive oil, and mustard. Taste and season with salt and pepper. Once thoroughly mixed, stir in half the truffles; save the rest for garnish.

3. Spoon the egg mixture into the halved egg whites on a large platter. Scatter the remaining truffles over the tops. Refrigerate the eggs and serve chilled.

SITTING ON THE DOCK OF THE BAY: From left, Ethan Domino, Zykia Strickland, Patrick Berrigan, Jack and Andrew Besh, Claire Berrigan.

POACHED EGGS & SATSUMA HOLLANDAISE OVER CRAB CAKES
Serves 8

This dish is much easier than it looks because you can make the crab cakes well in advance, browning them and keeping them on a baking sheet, ready to reheat moments before serving. Which leaves time to focus on the nuances of poaching the perfect egg. The satsuma hollandaise is an adaptation of a sauce called Sauce Maltaise made with blood oranges.

Satsumas, our local tangerines, were brought from Japan to Southern Louisiana by the Jesuits in the 18th century. The orchards they planted in nearby Plaquemines Parish thrive to this day. I love satsumas, but any kind of orange juice will work.

FOR THE CRAB CAKES
- 1 pound crabmeat, picked over
- 1 cup diced white bread
- ⅔ cup mayonnaise
- 2 green onions, chopped
- 2 dashes Tabasco
- Salt
- Freshly ground black pepper
- 3 cups bread crumbs
- ¼ cup canola oil

- 1 teaspoon coriander seeds
- Leaves from 1 sprig fresh thyme
- 1 bay leaf
- Juice of ½ lemon
- 4 egg yolks
- 1 cup hot clarified butter (between 135° and 145°)
- 1 pinch cayenne pepper
- Salt
- Tabasco

FOR THE HOLLANDAISE
- ½ cup satsuma or orange juice
- 1 tablespoon white wine vinegar
- 1 1-inch piece of ginger, peeled and crushed
- 1 shallot, minced
- 1 teaspoon black peppercorns

FOR THE POACHED EGGS
- 1 tablespoon white vinegar
- 1 teaspoon salt
- 8 eggs

1. For the crab cakes, gently mix together the crabmeat, diced bread, mayonnaise, and green onions in a bowl. Season with Tabasco, salt, and pepper. Put the bread crumbs in a shallow bowl. With your hands, gently form the crab mixture into 8 patties and carefully dredge in the bread crumbs.

2. Heat the canola oil in a skillet over medium heat. When the oil is hot, cook the crab cakes, in batches, until golden on both sides. Transfer to a baking sheet. The crab cakes may be cooled and refrigerated, then reheated or kept warm in a 200° oven.

3. For the hollandaise, combine the satsuma juice, vinegar, ginger, shallots, peppercorns, coriander, thyme, and bay leaf in a small saucepan over medium heat and boil until the liquid is reduced by half. Strain the reduction into a small bowl (discard the solids), whisk in the lemon juice, and let cool.

4. Pour the satsuma reduction over the egg yolks in a bowl and whisk well. Whisk in 1 tablespoon water. Place the bowl over a pot of simmering water, to make an improvised double boiler. Continue whisking the eggs over the hot water until they thicken and coat the back of a spoon, about 5 minutes. Remove from the heat.

5. Place the bowl on a secure surface or have someone hold the bowl as you continue to whisk the yolks while adding a slow, steady stream of hot clarified butter. When all the butter has been added, season with cayenne, salt, and Tabasco, and keep the sauce in a warm place near the stove.

6. Remove the crab cakes from the oven and transfer to a large serving platter.

7. For the poached eggs, combine 2½ cups water, the vinegar, and salt in a medium saucepan and bring to a boil. Lower the heat to a barely bubbling simmer. Crack each egg over the pot and gently lower it into the water. You can poach the eggs in batches. Cook the eggs for 3 minutes, remove with a slotted spoon, shaking off the water.

8. Place one poached egg on each crab cake. Drizzle the hollandaise over the top and serve.

FRUIT SALAD WITH CHAMPAGNE & MINT

Serves 8–10

This salad only works with the best local fruit. With fruit that fresh, almost any combination is great. Just toss the cut fruit with the Champagne and mint. It's the perfect way to begin a brunch—or to end it as a dessert. Even better, you can purée leftover fruit and freeze it for a delicious sorbet.

- 1 cup Champagne
- ¼ cup sugar
  Leaves from 2 sprigs fresh mint, minced
- 2 cups mixed berries (such as blueberries, blackberries, raspberries, strawberries)
- 2 cups diced melon (honeydew, cantaloupe, watermelon) or segmented citrus
- 1 cup sliced stone fruit (plums, nectarines, peaches)

1. Whisk together the Champagne, sugar, and mint in a small bowl.

2. Select a beautiful serving bowl and spoon in the berries and chopped fruit. Pour the Champagne mixture over the fruit and toss gently to mix.

LOUISIANA SATSUMA COCKTAIL

Serves 8

Jenifer, opposite, loves this version of the classic Mimosa, Champagne with orange juice. It uses tangerine juice from our local satsumas, but use any tangerines you can find.

- 1 bottle Champagne
- 2 cups fresh-squeezed satsuma or tangerine juice
- ½ cup arancello (Italian orange liqueur)

1. Pour the Champagne into a large pitcher. Add the tangerine juice and the arancello. Mix and serve chilled.

Smoothie Bar

SET OUT A TABLE with a blender (and an electric cord), carafes of fresh fruit juice such as orange, pineapple, grapefruit, and peach nectar. Load a tray with fresh fruit like bananas, pineapple, and fresh berries. Fill one bowl with plain yogurt and another with ice. Have kids mix and match their own smoothies, with the oldest (like Brendan, above) manning the blender.

ROASTED PEAR SALAD

Serves 8

You can roast just about any kind of pear, but for this recipe I prefer the smaller and harder Seckel pears. Once roasted, they'll soften and become surprisingly sweet and floral, a perfect contrast to the salty blue cheese and slightly bitter endive.

FOR THE PEARS

- 4 ripe pears, halved and cored
- 2 tablespoons olive oil
- 2 teaspoons sugar
  Salt

FOR THE VINAIGRETTE

- ½ cup olive oil
- ¼ cup pecan oil
- 3 tablespoons rice wine vinegar
- 1 tablespoon honey
- 1 teaspoon Creole mustard
- 1 shallot, minced
  Salt
  Freshly ground black pepper

FOR THE SALAD

- 5 heads Belgian endive, cored and leaves separated
- 2 handfuls mixed bitter green leaves
- 2 cups blue cheese, crumbled into chunks
- ½ cup pecans, toasted

1. For the pears, preheat the oven to 425°. In a small bowl, drizzle the pears with the olive oil, sprinkle with the sugar and salt, and toss to coat well. Transfer the pears to a baking sheet and roast for 10 minutes, until golden brown. Allow to cool.

2. For the vinaigrette, whisk together the olive oil, pecan oil, vinegar, honey, mustard, and shallots in a small mixing bowl. Season with salt and pepper.

3. To assemble the salad, combine the endive leaves and bitter greens in a large serving bowl. Add the vinaigrette and toss to coat well. Wait until just before serving to top with the pears, blue cheese, and pecans.

WARM ALSATIAN ONION TART

Serves 8

I absolutely love this deep-dish style onion tart for brunch, although it's often served throughout the day in Alsace. In a sense it's like a quiche, with just enough eggs to hold the onions and bacon together.

- 1 sheet frozen puff pastry, defrosted
- 1 cup large-diced slab bacon
- 3 onions, thinly sliced
- 1 clove garlic, minced
- ½ teaspoon caraway seeds
- 1 bay leaf
  Salt
  Freshly ground black pepper
- 4 eggs
- ½ cup milk

1. Preheat the oven to 325°. On a floured board, roll out the puff pastry until quite thin. Grease a deep 9-inch pie pan with soft butter, then dust with flour. Using the rolling pin to help transfer the pastry, fit the crust into the pie pan.

2. Cook the bacon in a medium saucepan over medium-high heat, stirring constantly, until the fat is rendered, about 5 minutes. Add the onions and stir for another 10 minutes, until the onions are caramelized. Add the garlic, caraway seeds, bay leaf, and a pinch of salt and pepper. Continue cooking and stirring for another 5 minutes, or until the onions have turned a deep mahogany brown. Discard the bay leaf.

3. In a mixing bowl, whisk together the eggs and milk. While stirring the eggs, add the warm bacon and onion mixture. Combine well and pour into the prepared pie shell. Bake for 35 minutes, or until the crust is browned and the center of the tart is set.

BLUE CRAB & SAUSAGE STEW

Serves 10

I love the smell of toasted crabs; the flavor of this stew will be greatly intensified if you sauté the crabs in a touch of oil first. Miss Gracie, the New Orleans cook who taught me to make this stew, only used beef sausage and, unlike other classic recipes, she never added butter at the end. However, now I use whatever sausage I have; see Resources, page 254.

¼ cup canola oil

5 jumbo blue crabs, quartered

1 large onion, diced

1 stalk celery, diced

1 bell pepper, seeded and diced

¼ cup flour

2 tablespoons tomato paste

2 cloves garlic, minced

2 quarts Shellfish Broth (page 26)

1 pound spicy smoked sausage links, sliced ½ inch thick

Leaves from 1 sprig fresh thyme

2 bay leaves

3 dashes Tabasco

2 dashes Worcestershire

Salt

Freshly ground black pepper

1 pound crabmeat, picked over

2 green onions, chopped

1 tablespoon butter

4–6 cups cooked Louisiana white rice

1. Heat the canola oil in a large heavy-bottomed pot over high heat. Throw in the crabs and toast, about 7 minutes a side, stirring. A beautiful aroma will fill the room.

2. Add the onions, celery, and bell peppers and continue to stir with a wooden spoon until softened, 3–5 minutes. Dust the flour over the ingredients in the pot, stirring constantly, and add the tomato paste and garlic. Stir for 2 minutes, making sure to scrape the bottom of the pot to keep the crabs from burning.

3. Add the shellfish broth and bring to a boil. Add the sausage, thyme, and bay leaves. Stir and lower the heat to medium low. Simmer for 15 minutes.

4. Season with Tabasco, Worcestershire, salt, and pepper. Add the crabmeat, green onions, and butter, stirring gently to mix well. Remove and discard the bay leaves. Serve the stew in bowls over rice.

STUFFED MUSHROOMS

Serves 8

You can make the stuffing a day ahead and even stuff the mushrooms, too. Refrigerate overnight, then, 30 minutes before you want to serve, drizzle the mushrooms with olive oil, sprinkle on a few bread crumbs, and pop into the oven to bake until brown and crisp.

2 tablespoons olive oil, plus more for drizzling

16 large button mushrooms, stems reserved and diced

½ onion, diced

1 stalk celery, diced

2 cloves garlic, minced

½ pound raw shrimp, peeled, deveined, and chopped

½ cup diced white bread

¾ cup bread crumbs

Salt

Freshly ground black pepper

¼ cup grated Parmesan cheese

1. Preheat the oven to 375°. For the stuffing, heat the oil in a large skillet over medium heat. Add the mushroom stems, onions, celery, and garlic and cook until softened, about 5 minutes. Add the shrimp and cook for an additional 3 minutes, stirring often. Stir in the diced bread and ½ cup of the bread crumbs and mix well. Season with salt and pepper. Remove from the heat and allow to cool.

2. Put the mushroom caps in a baking dish or on a baking sheet and fill each cap with a generous spoonful of shrimp stuffing. Drizzle the tops with a few drops of olive oil and sprinkle on the Parmesan cheese and the remaining ¼ cup bread crumbs. Bake for 15–20 minutes, until golden brown.

SUGAR SNAP PEA SALAD WITH PECANS

Serves 8

I like to find ways to expedite the prep of many of my recipes by doing as much as I can in advance. While I'll slice the sugar snaps ahead of time, I don't want to blanch them until just before serving so that they retain their beautiful color and crisp texture.

½ cup pecan halves	FOR THE VINAIGRETTE
2 tablespoons olive oil	¾ cup olive oil
Salt	¼ cup balsamic vinegar
1 pound sugar snap peas, ends snapped and strings removed, thinly sliced on the bias	1 clove garlic, minced
	Leaves from 1 sprig fresh basil, minced
	Salt
	Freshly ground black pepper

1. Preheat the oven to 325°. In a small bowl, drizzle the pecans with the olive oil and salt and toss to coat well. Scatter the pecans in a single layer on a baking sheet and bake for 15 minutes, or until golden brown and fragrant. Cool and reserve.

2. Bring a large pot of water to a boil over medium heat. Just before you're ready to serve, add the peas and cook for just 1 minute. With a slotted spoon, transfer the peas to a big bowl of ice water to stop the cooking and hold their color. Drain and place in a serving bowl.

3. For the vinaigrette, whisk together the olive oil, vinegar, garlic, and basil in a small bowl. Season with salt and pepper. Pour the vinaigrette over the peas and toss to coat. Sprinkle the toasted pecans over the top.

CRAB-STUFFED AVOCADOS

Serves 8

You can make the dressing for the crab salad in advance and pick the crab from the shells a day ahead, but don't combine the two or cut and fill the avocados until moments before you're ready to serve. The bright crab flavor will become muddled if seasoned in advance and cut avocados have a tendency to oxidize and darken.

1 cup mayonnaise	1 pinch cayenne pepper
Juice of 2 lemons	1½ teaspoons salt
¼ cup prepared horseradish	Freshly ground black pepper
2 teaspoons chopped fresh chives	1 pound jumbo lump crabmeat
2 teaspoons Dijon mustard	4 avocados, halved and pitted
1 teaspoon white wine vinegar	Baby greens for garnish

1. In a small bowl, whisk together the mayonnaise, lemon juice, horseradish, chives, mustard, vinegar, cayenne, salt, and pepper. Just before serving, gently fold the crabmeat into the mayonnaise mixture, being careful to not break up the lumps. Drop heaping spoonfuls of the crab into the avocados and scatter greens on top.

GARLICKY BAKED OYSTERS

Serves 6

The presentation alone of these baked oysters on the half shell (on the table beside Madeleine Berrigan, left) makes a great statement on a buffet table. Or you can can use freshly shucked oysters sold by the pint or quart, and assemble them in a large baking dish or in individual ramekins. Either way, be sure to get the flavorful oyster liquor. You can make the sauce and topping ahead and combine them at the last minute.

⅓ cup olive oil	1 cup bread crumbs
¼ cup white wine	1 cup grated Parmesan cheese
6 cloves garlic, thinly sliced	Leaves from 3 sprigs fresh thyme
1 tablespoon crushed red pepper flakes	3 dozen oysters on the half-shell, or 3 dozen shucked oysters, with their liquor
3 dashes Tabasco	
2 cups oyster liquor or Shellfish Broth (page 26)	

1. Preheat the oven to 500°. For the sauce, heat half the olive oil, the white wine, garlic, red pepper, and Tabasco in a small saucepan. Add the oyster liquor. Bring to a boil, then remove the pan from the heat.

2. For the topping, in a small bowl, mix the remaining olive oil with the bread crumbs, Parmesan, and thyme.

3. Place the oysters on the half shells on a baking sheet, or the shucked oysters in a large baking dish or in individual ramekins. Spoon the sauce over the oysters and add heaping spoonfuls of the topping. Bake for 5 minutes, or until the edges of the oysters begin to curl and the topping is golden brown and bubbly.

MARINATED CRAB FINGERS

Serves 8

If you can't find my beloved steamed blue crab claws for this dish, feel free to substitute stone crabs, Jonah crabs, or king crabs. When you toss any variety of boiled or steamed crab in a touch of vinaigrette you'll actually awaken their flavors.

1 cup olive oil	Few pinches Zatarain's Crab Boil or Old Bay seasoning
¼ cup rice wine vinegar	
2 tablespoons mayonnaise	2 dashes Tabasco
1 teaspoon horseradish	Salt
1 teaspoon lemon juice	Freshly ground black pepper
4 green onions, chopped	1 pound crab fingers
2 cloves garlic, minced	

1. Whisk together all of the ingredients for the marinade and toss with the crab fingers about 15 minutes before you're ready to serve.

CROWN ROAST OF PORK WITH DIRTY RICE DRESSING
Serves 8

A crown roast is a spectacular centerpiece for a large buffet spread. It's also pretty impressive when brought to a holiday table on a large platter. It is made with two racks of lamb, veal, or pork, tied together to form a circle. Ask your butcher to prepare and tie the pork racks for you, planning on one rib per person. Then assemble the stuffing, bake, and serve it forth! I just love rice dressing ("stuffing" to some of you) as it so reminds me of my childhood, its flavor reminiscent of our boudin sausages. As the pork roast renders and browns, the dressing will absorb all of its wonderful flavors.

FOR THE DRESSING

- 1 pound fresh pork sausage, casings removed
- 1 pound andouille sausage, chopped
- ¼ cup bacon drippings
- 1 onion, minced
- ½ cup chicken livers, chopped
- 1 stalk celery, minced
- 1 bell pepper, minced
- 4 green onions, chopped
- 2 cloves garlic, minced
- 1 teaspoon crushed red pepper flakes
- 2 cups uncooked jasmine rice
- 1 teaspoon pimentón
- 4 cups chicken broth
  Salt
  Freshly ground black pepper

FOR THE CROWN ROAST

- 1 pork crown roast, tied
- 2 tablespoons butter, softened
  Leaves from 1 sprig fresh thyme
  Salt
  Freshly ground black pepper

1. Preheat the oven to 375°. For the dressing, brown the pork sausage and andouille sausage in the bacon drippings in a heavy skillet over high heat, stirring constantly. Once the sausage meat has browned, add the onions and continue stirring for another 3–5 minutes, then add the chicken livers. Make sure the livers have a chance to cook for a minute or two. Then add the celery, bell peppers, green onions, garlic, and pepper flakes and cook until soft.

2. Add the rice and pimentón and stir well so that the grains of rice are coated with the fat. Add the chicken broth and bring to a boil over high heat. Once boiling, cover the pan with a lid, reduce the heat to low, and cook for 15 minutes. Season with salt and pepper.

3. For the crown roast, rub the roast inside and out with soft butter and season generously with thyme, salt, and pepper. Place the roast in a deep roasting pan and fill the center with the rice dressing. Wrap the ends of each rib bone with foil to prevent burning. Secure with butcher's string. Cook for 1 hour, or until the pork roast reaches 145° on a meat thermometer and is a deep honey brown.

4. Remove the string from the roast, slice and serve one chop per person along with some succulent dressing.

JEWEL IN THE CROWN: The prize is, of course, that tasty rice dressing pressed inside the "crown" of pork ribs that your butcher will be happy to prepare. Have him "French" the ribs, which means strip them, for a fine presentation. Then tie the ribs again, left, securing the stuffing.

"The fragrant smoke from wood-burning fireplaces…

permeates the crisp mountain air and mixes with the scents of tannenbaum, juniper, and laurel. A ringing bell and shouts of "Glühwein" and "vin chaud" at the market are signs that Christmas is near in this secluded village in the Black Forest. These sounds remind me how very far away from home I am. The mountains have long been covered with snow, and the short days have long since turned gray, but the mood around the Christmas fair, the Weihnachtsmarkt, is gleefully joyous.

HOLIDAY BIRDS: The painterly still life of red cabbage and onion, above, will soon become a braise under our holiday goose. My boys Andrew and Luke, opposite, hold two splendid wild birds hunted by their Uncle Patrick, while I show off a domestic version complete with dumplings.

Neighbors who never smile seem today to grin just a bit, and the postman, who always looks troubled by me, gives me the ole "Grüss Gott," God is good. Sabine, the chef's wife, walks the forest with her children, gathering small twigs that they paint and turn into the most imaginative mobiles to decorate the Romantik Hotel Spielweg. Branches of tannenbaum are twisted into every imaginable shape, to fill each room with green life. Fires crackle and hiss in the fireplaces throughout the old guest house, their soft flickering light illuminating the rooms and offering much needed respite from the bracingly frigid temperatures outside.

The children will be spoiled today with gifts of chocolate and impeccably wrapped toys. Chocolate is the universal gift on St. Nicholas Day, and perhaps that's why the Germans are so happy. Or could it be the Glühwein—the sensuous drink of hot spiced wine mellowed with cinnamon, allspice, and bay leaves—that warms them from the inside out? The mood becomes more joyous as fruit brandy, added to the Glühwein for another hit of alcohol, takes effect. It's easy to confuse the aroma of roasted cherries with that of the fortified wine. But when I look closely, I notice that pans full of dried cherry pits have been heating in the oven for several hours and are now being carefully poured into small cloth cases. Once all the cases are filled, they're placed into the bed of each hotel guest, so that after dinner when the guests retire they'll find their beds warmed by fragrant pillows of cherry pits.

The Stammtisch—the family table in the dining room that has been in constant use since the 1730s—feels as if it had been set for just Jenifer and me. It's quite an honor to be invited to sit at this table and very much unheard of for the chef, Karl-Josef Fuchs, my boss, to invite a young cook and his wife to holiday dinner with his family.

This is to be my first Christmas goose and it isn't even Christmas yet. St. Nicholas Day, on December 6, is the true beginning of the Christmas season in Germany and is often celebrated with more tradition than the big day itself. Goose is on the menu and there is no question that I will learn how to cook it, under the direction of Karl-Josef, with the gentle prodding of his beautiful mother, Josefine, and all to the amusement of Hans-Jörg, his jolly, larger-than-life father. Soon the chef's brothers will arrive with their families, just as they always do.

How to Cook Your Goose

UNTIL ST. NICHOLAS DAY in the Black Forest of Germany, the only geese I'd ever cooked were the wild ones of my youth, the speckled belly goose, blue goose, snow goose, and the lesser Canada goose that spend the winter in South Louisiana. The goose that I was to cook that day was quite large and fattened beyond recognition on one of the farms in the Münster Valley, a whole different animal from the wild geese I knew; snowy white fat under its thick skin insulated the dark flesh of the plump breast. Such a bird needs to be cooked slowly, taking great care to let the fat render and crisp the skin. In essence, the bird is cooked so that it confits in its own skin. The bird's breast and legs have to cook long and slow until the drumstick can be twisted. No matter what the bird weighs, I've found that twisting is the best way to determine whether it's done.

The geese I love to cook today are similarly farm-raised, fat, and tender. I make sure to get mine a few days ahead and leave it unseasoned and unwrapped in the refrigerator for a day or two, so that it dries out a bit. I season it well with salt and pepper inside and out. In the cavity of the bird, I put a halved garlic head, a few shallots, and a handful of fresh thyme branches. Then I trim the wings and tie the legs of that magnificent bird. Once the goose is bound with butcher's string, I rub it with soft farmers' butter, season it liberally with salt and cracked black pepper, and sprinkle it all over with fresh-picked thyme, watching the leaves drift and adhere to the sticky butter. Then I transfer the goose to a roasting pan layered with diced onions, celery, and carrots, and the bird's wings too. I add water to the vegetables in the pan, slide it into the oven, and let the bird slowly roast. I watch as the goose becomes golden, and then mahogany brown.

When the bird is done, I move it to a vast serving platter to await carving. When the goose is served, it will be accompanied by sweet and velvety red cabbage slow-cooked with apples and onions, and yellow potatoes transformed into pillowy dumplings stuffed with rendered bacon, croutons, and chives. As I remove (and save) the precious goose fat from the roasting pan, the vegetables and pan drippings will become the luscious sauce for perhaps the most perfect meal of the year.

POTATO LATKES

Serves 4

A little something special about making potato pancakes: you must work quickly so the potatoes don't oxidize. I like to have everything ready before I begin. Once I grate the potatoes and onions, there will be liquid in the bowl. I use my fingers to remove the potato mixture from the liquid, squeezing to shake the water away. I take my time to make sure the pancakes are really crunchy, first forming and pre-cooking them and then freezing them. Just before serving, I fry them again so they're really crispy. The beautiful fall-colored fruit compote, left, is a perfect accompaniment.

2 large egg whites	¼ teaspoon freshly ground black pepper
1 pound (2–3 medium sized) Yukon Gold potatoes, peeled	Canola oil, for frying
¼ white onion	Fall Fruit Compote (recipe left), or sour cream and chopped fresh dill
2 tablespoons flour	
1½ teaspoons kosher salt	

1. In a large mixing bowl, beat the egg whites with a whisk until frothy. Using a box grater, coarsely shred the potatoes and onions. Squeeze and drain well and add to the beaten egg whites. Fold in the flour, salt, and pepper and mix gently but well.

2. In a large non-stick skillet, heat 1 tablespoon canola oil. Form small pancakes, about 3 inches in diameter, in the pan. Cook over medium heat, turning once, until golden brown, 3–5 minutes on each side. With a spatula, transfer the latkes to a baking sheet. Repeat with the remaining potato mixture. When the latkes are cooled, cover and transfer to the freezer.

3. When ready to serve the latkes, heat ¼ inch oil in a non-stick skillet. Return the latkes to the oil in batches and cook a second time for 3–4 minutes, turning, until both sides are deep amber brown and crispy. Remove from the pan and drain on paper towels. Serve with the Fall Fruit Compote or sour cream and dill.

FALL FRUIT COMPOTE

Makes about 2 cups

1 tablespoon butter	¼ cup apple cider vinegar
2 Honeycrisp apples, cored and diced	¼ cup apple juice
2 pears, cored and diced	¼ cup brown sugar
½ cup dried cherries, chopped	1 cinnamon stick

1. Melt the butter in a medium saucepan over high heat. Add the diced apples, pears, cherries, vinegar, apple juice, brown sugar, and cinnamon stick. Cook for 5 minutes. Lower the heat to medium and cook a few minutes more, until the fruit is tender and the liquid has boiled away. Add a bit more apple juice to keep the fruit from scorching. The compote will keep for a week, refrigerated. Serve warm with potato latkes.

COUNTRY-STYLE CHICKEN & GOOSE LIVER PÂTÉ

Serves 10

This is about the easiest, tastiest pâté I know. If you don't have goose fat from roasting a goose, don't worry. Butter works wonderfully as a replacement.

2	cups goose and chicken livers	1	tablespoon salt
2	eggs	1	pinch ground white pepper
1½	teaspoons celery salt	1½	cups hot goose fat and/or warmed butter
1½	teaspoons garlic powder		
1½	teaspoons onion powder		

1. Preheat the oven to 300°. Combine the livers, eggs, celery salt, garlic powder, onion powder, salt, and white pepper in a blender jar. While blending, pour the hot fat slowly into the mixture. Continue to blend until everything is incorporated and very smooth. Strain through a fine-mesh sieve into a pâté mold or baking dish.

2. Set the baking dish into a larger pan filled with hot water to come halfway up the sides of the baking dish. Bake in this water bath for 30–45 minutes, until the pâté is set. Remove and refrigerate for about 2 hours before serving. Serve with thinly sliced toasts.

BRAISED RED CABBAGE WITH APPLES & ONIONS

Serves 10

I love this simple cabbage dish in the winter. It is luscious and velvety and works with almost any roast. If you don't have rendered bacon fat on hand, just chop up some bacon and cook it to render the fat, leaving in the bits of bacon. This is one of those dishes that will only improve if made a day or two in advance and reheated.

¼	cup bacon fat	⅓	cup red wine vinegar
1	red onion, sliced	2	juniper berries, crushed
2	cloves garlic, minced	1	bay leaf
1	head red cabbage, cored and thinly sliced	1	pinch ground cloves
2	apples, cored and diced		Salt
½	cup sugar		Freshly ground black pepper

1. Heat the bacon fat in a heavy-bottomed pan over medium-high heat. Add the onions and garlic and sweat until the onions are translucent. Add the cabbage, apples, sugar, vinegar, juniper berries, bay leaf, and cloves. Stir frequently for 5 minutes, until the cabbage begins to wilt. Reduce the heat to medium low and let the cabbage cook for about 35 minutes, stirring occasionally. When the cabbage becomes completely tender and slightly sweet, discard the bay leaf, season with salt and pepper, and it's ready to serve.

CREAMY LENTIL SOUP

Serves 8

I learned about this soup in Germany, where it was often served as a midday break for hunters, or at midnight for drinkers! I've added cream to this recipe, which I've never seen before in a lentil soup. It gives the soup such a succulent texture.

1 cup diced bacon	Leaves from 2 sprigs fresh thyme
1 onion, diced small	2 dashes cayenne pepper
¼ cup minced carrot	1 bay leaf
¼ cup minced celery stalk or celery root	2 cups cream
2 cloves garlic, minced	Salt
1 pound dried French green lentils	Freshly ground black pepper

1. In a heavy-bottomed pot over medium-high heat, cook the bacon until the fat is rendered and the pieces are golden brown. Add the onions, carrots, celery, and garlic and sweat until the vegetables are soft, about 5 minutes.

2. Add the lentils, thyme, cayenne, bay leaf, and enough water to cover by 2 inches. Bring to a boil over high heat, then reduce the heat to medium low and simmer gently for 1 hour.

3. Once the lentils are tender, add the cream, raise the heat to medium high, and cook for an additional 15 minutes. Discard the bay leaf. Taste and season with salt and pepper before serving.

GOOSE LESSONS: First I take the goose that has dried out in the refrigerator and cut off the wings and save them for a rack in the pan with the vegetables. I season the cavity, stuff it with garlic and herbs, then tie the legs with butcher's string.

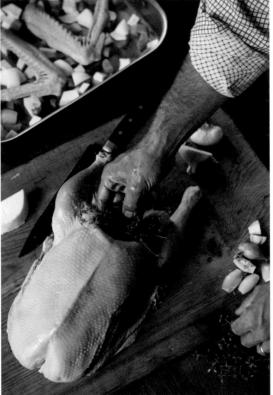
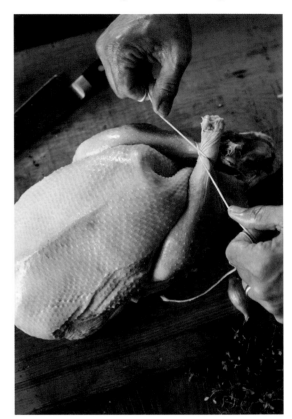

ROAST GOOSE

Serves 10

It takes patience to cook a goose, for there's only one right way and that is low and slow. The point is to gradually render all of the luscious fat beneath the skin, which will baste the bird throughout the cooking process. A goose is self-basting! The best thing is that you're left with incredible pan drippings, including valuable tasty goose fat. I separate most of the fat from the drippings and save it along with the liver for my pâté (page 215). The wings and vegetables in the bottom of the pan act as a natural roasting rack for the goose, plus they add big-time flavor to the sauce.

1 8–10-pound goose	2 carrots, diced
Salt	2 stalks celery, diced
Freshly ground black pepper	2 tablespoons butter, softened
1 head garlic, halved	Leaves from 3 sprigs fresh thyme
2 shallots, peeled and halved	3 tablespoons flour
Several fresh thyme branches	2 cups chicken broth
2 onions, diced	Butcher's string

1. Preheat the oven to 350°. Cut the wings off the goose at the elbow joint and set aside; you'll need them later. Season the bird liberally inside with salt and pepper and stuff the garlic head, shallots, and thyme branches inside.

MORE GOOSE LESSONS: I salt the goose, then rub it all over with soft butter, and salt and pepper the skin. I've carefully picked the fresh thyme leaves off their branches and now I scatter them over the buttered goose so they'll stick.

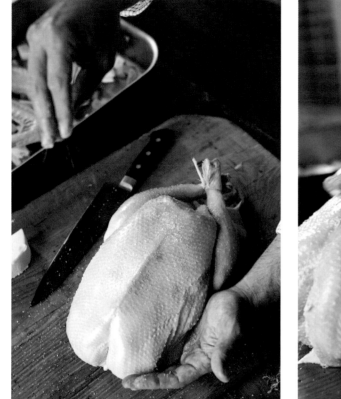
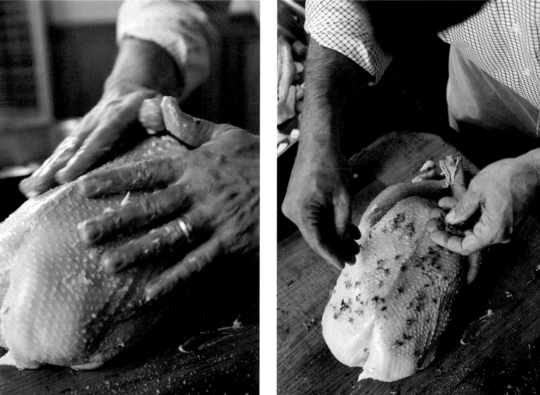

2. Tie the legs together with butcher's string, securing the flavor-giving garlic and herbs inside.

3. Scatter the onions, carrots, and celery in a heavy-bottomed roasting pan. Arrange the wing ends to make a flavorful rack for the goose. Lay the goose on top, season with salt and pepper, and rub all over with the butter. Sprinkle the exterior liberally with the thyme leaves. Add enough water to the pan to cover the bottom by ½ inch.

4. Roast the goose for 4 hours, or until the skin turns amber and the drumstick twists easily in its socket. Carefully remove the pan from the oven and gently transfer the bird to a large serving platter.

5. For the sauce, pour the pan drippings, including the vegetables, into a large measuring cup and wait for the fat to rise to the top. Separate the fat from the drippings.

6. Put 3 tablespoons of the fat into a medium saucepan over a high heat. With a wooden spoon, mix in the flour and stir vigorously until the flour is evenly browned. Once the roux is brown, whisk in the chicken broth and remaining pan drippings. Bring the sauce to a boil, reduce the heat, and simmer slowly for 15 minutes. Remove the sauce from the heat and pass it through a fine mesh strainer. Season with salt and pepper and serve with the goose.

OUR HOLIDAY TABLE: Be it Thanksgiving or Christmas (and a goose is perfect for both), instead of fussy centerpieces, we scatter pomegranates and other fresh fruit on the table, and always lots of candlelight. The holiday plate, right, with braised cabbage, luscious potato dumplings, and a perfect serving of roast goose.

YUKON GOLD POTATO DUMPLINGS
Serves 8

Imagine these as fluffy, tender, and delicious potato meatballs. I say that because forming them into balls with wet hands is as easy as shaping meatballs. When you stuff each dumpling with bacon, you create a delicious surprise for your guests. I make these at least once a year as a tribute to my first roast goose dinner. Once cooked, they will hold in the water in the pot with the heat turned off for up to 20 minutes.

2	pounds Yukon Gold potatoes	¾	cup flour
	Salt	2	medium eggs
1	cup diced bacon		Freshly grated nutmeg
1	cup diced rustic bread		Freshly ground white pepper
1	tablespoon chopped fresh chives	1	cup (2 sticks) butter
		¾	cup bread crumbs

1. Rinse the potatoes and place in a 1-gallon pot. Cover with water and season with 2 tablespoons salt. Bring to a boil over high heat. Reduce to a simmer and cook until the potatoes are fork tender. Remove the potatoes from the water and let them cool slightly. With a paring knife, gently peel the warm potatoes; the peels will pull away easily from the potatoes once they are cooled. Place the potatoes in a large mixing bowl.

2. While the potatoes are cooking, cook the bacon in a medium skillet over medium-high heat until the fat is rendered and the pieces turn golden. Add the diced bread and stir until all the pieces are evenly browned. With a slotted spoon, remove the bacon and croutons from the pan and drain on paper towels. In a small bowl, mix the bacon and croutons with the chopped chives. Refrigerate until needed.

3. Place another large pot of salted water on the stove to cook the dumplings and bring to a gentle simmer.

Using a potato ricer, process the peeled potatoes into a mixing bowl. Add the flour and eggs and mix well. Season with ½ teaspoon salt, a pinch of nutmeg, and white pepper to taste. The potato dough should be slightly sticky, but still hold a shape. If the mixture seems very loose, add a bit more flour.

4. To roll the dumplings, set out a bowl of warm water to dip your hands into occasionally to keep the dough from sticking. Flatten a generous tablespoon-sized portion of dough in the palm of one hand. In the center of the dough, place a teaspoon of the bacon and crouton mixture. Slowly begin closing your hand and the dough around the filling, while molding and shaping the dough with the fingertips of your other hand. You want to gently bring the outside of the dough together into a ball, molding and smoothing with the other hand. Once the ball is sealed, roll it between the palms of both hands into a perfect sphere. Repeat to make more dumplings.

5. Carefully drop the dumplings into the pot of simmering salted water, all at once. Allow the dumplings to poach very slowly for 10 minutes. They'll rise to the surface in minutes, but they need the extra simmering to make sure they're fully cooked in the center. You can proceed with the recipe or hold the dumplings in the pot of water for 20 minutes.

6. While the dumplings are poaching, warm the butter and bread crumbs together in a small skillet. Season with salt and keep warm.

7. Remove dumplings from water with a slotted spoon and transfer to a large platter. Top each dumpling with some of the warmed buttery bread crumbs and serve.

HANDIWORK: Making potato dumplings is a bit of a skill but so much fun. Here, Mike Gulotta, chef at our Restaurant August, shows us how a pro does it.

MULLED CIDER

Serves 12

This warm, gently spiced cider smells like Christmas and is so easy to make, with or without the apple brandy. If you can find a good German or Alsatian schnapps, substitute that because the flavors work beautifully together.

2 quarts fresh apple cider	1 bay leaf
2 tablespoons sugar	1 whole clove
12 strips orange zest, made with a vegetable peeler	2 shots apple brandy, optional
1 stick cinnamon	

1. Pour the cider into a large pot and add the sugar, orange zest, cinnamon, bay leaf, and clove. Bring to a simmer for 1 minute, but do not boil.

2. Remove from the heat, add the brandy or schnapps if you like, and ladle into cups or mugs with a strip of orange zest in each.

SPIELWEG CHOCOLATE TORTE

Serves 8

By now everyone has heard of flourless chocolate cake. My version of the Romantik Hotel Spielweg's specialty is a luxuriously rich cake that's barely held together with a bit of flour. The eggs give it a silky texture. It's perfect when made a day or two in advance.

8 ounces dark chocolate	**FOR THE GANACHE**
¾ cup (1½ sticks) unsalted butter	6 ounces dark chocolate
6 eggs	½ cup plus 2 tablespoons cream
1 cup granulated sugar	1 tablespoon butter
½ cup all-purpose flour, sifted	
	¼ cup shaved white chocolate for garnish

1. Preheat the oven to 350°. Grease a 9-inch round cake pan with butter and dust with flour. Set a stainless steel mixing bowl over a pot of boiling water to make a double boiler. Melt the dark chocolate with the butter in the bowl. Remove from the heat and set aside.

2. In another mixing bowl, beat the eggs and sugar with a handheld mixer until well combined. Slowly add the flour. Once the flour is combined, add the warmed dark chocolate/butter mixture in a slow steady stream, using a rubber spatula to incorporate.

3. Scrape the batter into the prepared pan. Set the pan into a larger pan filled with hot water to come halfway up the sides of the cake pan. Bake the cake in this water bath for 30 minutes, or until firm in the center. Remove from the water bath and let cool for 15 minutes.

4. For the ganache, melt the chocolate, cream, and butter in a heavy-bottomed saucepan over medium heat and mix until well combined. Remove from the heat and set aside.

5. Carefully remove the torte from the pan and transfer to a cake stand. Slowly pour the ganache over the torte so that it coats the top and all sides. When the torte is cool, mound the shaved white chocolate in the center of the glistening torte.

Drew Makes a Cake
(& Other Desserts)

"His curly blonde hair is as wild and unruly when he wakes up…

in the morning as it is when he falls into bed at night. His smile is wide and genuine. Never have I imagined eyes that really do twinkle like Andrew's do. Of our four boys, he's the eater, with an appetite for all things food and an appetite for life to match. Drew is wildly lovable. He knows no half throttle, only full speed ahead. I love late spring days with Drew, because he's a morning person just like me. The moment he wakes up he's ready for action. In spring-time, action means the blue-berry bushes and blackberry brambles outside our door.

Don't misunderstand: I'm not playing favorites. Jack's pretty good in the mornings, too, as is Luke, but both would much rather someone else do the picking; they'll take care of the eating part. If Brendan, the teenager, had it his way we wouldn't even see him until sometime around noon.

Most mornings, I'm in the kitchen drinking a coffee when Drew begins his ritual. He predictably pops out from around a corner to scare me and I predictably jump, startled. When he asks, "What's for bregfest, Daddy?" I reply with the same litany of stuff I make every day. Then he runs out the side door in search of berries. Not five minutes later, he reappears, mouth stained purple, and presents his bowl full of berries and asks, "Daddy, you gonna bake a cake with me and my berries?" And I've done this enough to know Drew means a cobbler, not a cake.

Each of our four boys is so very different; each is so beautiful. But they are quite competitive. Ever since Jack claimed that he was the first one to bake a cake, Drew became determined to not just to bake the cake but to supply the berries, too. Cobblers are so easy to put together and the ones I like the most really do resemble a cake. The cobbler is a good starter dessert for Andrew. He'll whip one up, pop it in the oven for 20 minutes, and it's done. Have I mentioned the Besh boys don't have much patience? Other cakes take too long and for that you need Jack or Luke. Brendan has the concentration for baking, but have I mentioned he's a teenager?

Pies would be just as easy, but take longer to bake and cool which makes them more suitable for Luke. Pies also require working the dough, just the excuse Luke needs to get his hands dirty. Besh boys are never happy unless something's getting dirty. Luke's pie recipes are quite forgiving, so when he adds a bit more of this or that, it probably won't matter. Jack is a boy's boy who's at times consumed by his wild, thrill-seeking side: bananas flambé suits him perfectly. Brendan, unlike his Dad, is the rule follower. So you do want him on the cakes. If you say "measure" then he'll measure, and it's that precision mentality that makes an accomplished baker. My mother, Imelda, is like that. She's a heck of a baker and draws a huddle of grandchildren around her every time she sets foot in our kitchen.

We don't buy processed desserts, cakes, or cookies—which is the way I was raised. If my lads want sweets, well, we'll have to bake them ourselves. It amazes me just how many things we can learn from baking: the discipline of measuring exactly, the math involved in fractions, the focus to understand each ingredient and how it reacts—all are great lessons.

I can see so much of myself in my boys today. When I was nine or so, a great tragedy struck our family. My father was seriously injured in a bicycling accident and my grandmother moved into our house to help. It was baking with her that calmed me. Happiness was smelling the deep aroma of caramelized brown sugar in her oatmeal cookies. Perhaps one day, the smell of baking will bring my boys back to their childhood, too. One thing is for certain, every time I bake with Drew, Luke, Jack, or Brendan, I can't help but think: these are the best of times. Family and friends gathered around, cooking, eating, drinking, and talking. I know this is as good as it gets; these just might be the best times we've ever spent doing anything.

BESH BOYS BAKING: Getting Brendan, opposite, our teenager and the oldest, to appear before noon on a weekend is an achievement, but he's great at fruit crumbles. Luke, below opposite, is a natural cookie maker. Jack, left, has the concentration to fill Black Forest Cupcakes with sweet cherries, while Drew, top, has been out berry picking since the crack of dawn.

Thoughts on Dessert

I GREW UP IN A HECTIC HOUSE with four sisters, one brother, one Great Santini father, and a mother who kept our household together and nourished us with her baking. We never ate store-bought desserts, but there was always a jar filled with incredible chocolate chip and oatmeal cookies. No frozen pies either, but we always looked forward to a pecan or icebox pie after school. It's in this homey spirit that I created the desserts in this chapter.

Dessert at home requires fine ingredients, a little bit of planning, and a whole lot of heart. The scrumptious results will feed the stomach and the soul in a way that restaurant desserts often attempt but don't always achieve. The pastry shops in our restaurants are full of talented, artisanal chefs who meticulously invent their impressive delectables. But to be honest, very little of what they do applies to the home cook. However, one crucial takeaway from our pastry kitchens is the sourcing of great ingredients: farmstead butters, wholesome hen eggs raised by someone who cares, and heavy cream and good milk that are hormone- and antibiotic-free and fed on good grass just as God intended. From these I make custard—the simple and versatile combination of eggs with sugar and milk in any form, that then becomes ice creams and crème brûlées. Remarkably enough, these pure ingredients are easier to find today than they were a mere ten years ago.

Baking at home, I only have time for quick breads with baking powder and treats like our cupcakes and Hummingbird Cake. Pie dough, though easy enough, is a bit messy. So when I am making dough for a pie, I'll prepare several batches, roll out the crusts, and wrap them in plastic wrap for the freezer. This way a piecrust is always at my fingertips.

The important thing about making desserts at home is to have fun. All that measuring and weighing can be tedious, so don't get overambitious. And remember that pastry can't be rushed. Assess how much time you have to devote to a dish before trying to conquer it and plan accordingly. Take cupcakes. You may wish to make the filling a day or so in advance, keeping the baking enjoyable by having everything ready to go. Some other desserts can be done almost entirely ahead so that you need only assemble the finished dish just before serving. And, of course, many desserts are best done quickly, like our Bananas Flambé, which takes no time at all and must be eaten just out of the skillet.

OATMEAL–CHOCOLATE CHIP COOKIES

Makes 16–20

This cookie dough can be made in advance, rolled in plastic wrap, and frozen until you're ready to make the cookies. To bake the frozen dough, just cut cookies off the roll.

- 1 cup (2 sticks) butter, softened
- 1 cup packed light brown sugar
- ½ cup granulated sugar
- 2 eggs
- 2 teaspoons vanilla extract
- 1¼ cups all-purpose flour
- ½ teaspoon baking powder
- 2 teaspoons salt
- 3 cups quick-cooking oats
- 1 12-ounce package (2 cups) semisweet chocolate chips
- 1½ cups chopped walnuts

1. Preheat the oven to 325°. In a large bowl, cream together the butter, brown sugar, and granulated sugar with a handheld mixer until smooth. Beat in the eggs one at a time, then add the vanilla.

2. In another bowl, sift together the flour, baking powder, and salt; stir into the creamed mixture until just blended. Mix in the oats, chocolate chips, and walnuts until just incorporated. Use an ice cream scoop (as Luke does here), to form cookies or drop by spoonfuls onto ungreased baking sheets.

3. Bake the cookies for 12 minutes until the edges begin to brown. Cool cookies on baking sheets and then transfer to a wire rack to cool completely.

GINGERSNAPS

Makes 16–20

I like to portion my cookie dough with a small ice cream scooper, then roll out the scoops into rounds for nice, even-sized cookies. If you don't have a scooper, use two teaspoons to shape the batter.

¾ cup (1½ sticks) butter	1 tablespoon ground ginger
1½ cups sugar	
1 egg	1 teaspoon cinnamon
¼ cup molasses	¼ teaspoon cardamom
2 cups all-purpose flour	½ teaspoon salt
2 teaspoons baking powder	

1. Preheat the oven to 350°. In a large mixing bowl, cream together the butter and 1 cup of the sugar with a handheld mixer until smooth. Beat in the egg and molasses until well blended. Sift together the flour, baking powder, ginger, cinnamon, cardamom, and salt into a bowl. Gently fold the flour mixture into the molasses mixture.

2. Place the remaining ½ cup sugar on a plate. Use a small ice cream scoop to portion the dough into about 18 pieces. On a lightly floured surface, roll each piece into a small circle. Dip one side of each round in the sugar and place 3–4 inches apart, sugar side up, on ungreased baking sheets.

3. Bake the cookies for 8–10 minutes. Let the cookies cool slightly on the baking sheets and transfer to a cooling rack.

SNICKERDOODLES

Makes 16–20

The dough for these cinnamon sugar cookies can be made and refrigerated in a closed container for up to 3 days before baking. Or, it can be frozen until you're ready to bake the cookies.

½ cup (1 stick) butter, softened	2¾ cups all-purpose flour
½ cup shortening	2 teaspoons cream of tartar
1½ cups plus 3 tablespoons sugar	1 teaspoon baking soda
2 eggs	½ teaspoon salt
2 teaspoons vanilla extract	2 teaspoons cinnamon

1. Preheat the oven to 350°. In a large mixing bowl, cream together the butter, shortening, the 1½ cups sugar, eggs, and vanilla. In a separate bowl, sift together the flour, cream of tartar, baking soda, and salt. Fold the flour mixture into the butter mixture until just incorporated. Shape the dough into 2-inch balls.

2. Mix the remaining 3 tablespoons sugar with the cinnamon and spread on a plate. Roll the dough balls in the cinnamon sugar and place 3 inches apart on ungreased baking sheets.

3. Bake the cookies for 8–10 minutes, until the edges begin to brown. Transfer cookies onto a cooling rack.

HOME SWEETS HOME:
House favorites, from left, Brendan's Apple & Pear Crumble, Black Forest Cupcakes above Brown Butter–Molasses Cupcakes. Three portions of Warm Any Fruit Crumble sit beneath Hummingbird Cake, perched properly on a pedestal. Then comes Lemon-Blackberry Cheesecake and a plate of yummy cookies: Gingersnaps, Oatmeal–Chocolate Chip, and Snickerdoodles.

LEMON-BLACKBERRY CHEESECAKE
Serves 8

This two-layer cheesecake looks cool and tastes better. It is nice to see the pure cheesecake layer above the berries, but if you're in a rush you really don't need to divide the batter; just add the purée and berries to the entire batter and omit that step.

3 tablespoons butter, softened	1 cup sour cream
1 cup graham cracker crumbs	¼ cup all-purpose flour
2 pounds cream cheese	1 tablespoon vanilla extract
1½ cups sugar	1½ pints blackberries
¾ cup milk	Zest and juice of 1 lemon
4 eggs	

1. Preheat the oven to 350°. Grease a 9-inch springform pan with 1 tablespoon of the butter. Mix the graham cracker crumbs with the remaining 2 tablespoons butter in a medium bowl. Press onto the bottom and halfway up the sides of the pan.

2. In a large bowl, use a handheld mixer to combine the cream cheese with the sugar until smooth. Blend in the milk, then beat in the eggs one at a time, mixing just enough to incorporate. Mix in the sour cream, flour, and vanilla until smooth. Divide the mixture between two bowls.

3. In a food processor or blender, purée 1 pint of the blackberries with the lemon zest and juice. Pour the purée into one bowl of the cheese mixture along with the remaining ½ pint of whole blackberries and mix well.

4. Pour the blackberry filling on top of the prepared crust. Bake for 10 minutes. Remove the pan from the oven and pour the remaining filling over the top. Return to the oven to bake for 1 hour, until the topping is set. Chill in the refrigerator until ready to serve.

CRÈME BRÛLÉE
Serves 8

Crème brûlée is probably the best-selling restaurant dessert ever because people think it's too difficult to make at home. But this custard with crispy melted sugar on top is really easy. One of the best ways to caramelize the sugar topping is to use a handheld torch, available at many cooking supply stores. And of course there's always the broiler.

2 tablespoons butter	1 vanilla bean, split
1 quart heavy cream	10 egg yolks
1¼ cups sugar	

1. Preheat the oven to 350°. Use the butter to grease eight 3-inch ramekins and set aside. In a medium saucepan over medium-high heat, combine the cream, 1 cup of the sugar, and the vanilla bean. Bring to a boil, stirring until the sugar dissolves. Once the cream comes to a boil, remove from the heat and let steep for 5 minutes. Remove the vanilla bean.

2. In a mixing bowl, beat the egg yolks with a whisk and slowly add the warm cream mixture until well blended. Pour the custard into the prepared ramekins and set into a larger metal pan. Fill the outer pan with hot water to come halfway up the sides of the ramekins. Bake the custards in this water bath for 30–40 minutes, until the custards have set in the center.

3. Carefully remove the pan from the oven and the ramekins from the pan. Let the custards cool completely. Just before serving, top each ramekin with a couple of spoonfuls of the remaining sugar. Caramelize the sugar until it melts, darkens, and covers the custards completely, either by placing the ramekins on a baking sheet and sliding it under the broiler, or using a handheld torch.

RICE PUDDING CRÈME BRÛLÉE

Serves 6

I love to use aromatic rice in this version of a classic crème brûlée, especially basmati, jasmine, or even popcorn rice from Crowley, Louisiana.

6 tablespoons butter	2 cups uncooked aromatic rice
2 cups milk	1 cup granulated sugar
Zest of 1 orange	4 large egg yolks
1 teaspoon vanilla extract	½ cup raw sugar or brown sugar for topping
1 teaspoon cinnamon	
½ teaspoon salt	

1. Preheat the oven to 325°. With 2 tablespoons of the butter, generously grease the sides of a large baking dish and set aside. In a medium saucepan over medium heat, combine the milk, orange zest, vanilla, cinnamon, and salt and bring to a boil. Add the rice and cook for about 30 minutes.

2. Meanwhile, in a large mixing bowl, cream the remaining 4 tablespoons butter and the granulated sugar until light and fluffy. Add the egg yolks one at a time, incorporating well after each addition.

3. Carefully fold the rice mixture into the egg mixture and pour into the prepared baking dish. Set the baking dish into a larger metal pan. Fill the outer pan with hot water to come halfway up the sides of the baking dish. Bake the custard in this water bath until just set, about 30 minutes. Carefully remove from the oven.

4. Rice pudding should be served hot with a crispy top. To serve, sprinkle the top generously with the raw or brown sugar and caramelize under the broiler or with a handheld torch.

BRENDAN'S APPLE & PEAR CRUMBLE

Serves 8

I know I said Brendan likes to bake and although he usually doesn't have the time, this easy version of our Warm Any Fruit Crumble (page 22) appeals to his over-crowded schedule. You can make the crumble with apples, pears, or a combination. Add a peeled and chopped quince if you can find one.

3 cups chopped cored peeled apples and/or pears, 3–4 whole fruits	**FOR THE TOPPING**
	⅔ cup all-purpose flour
3 tablespoons brown sugar	⅓ cup packed brown sugar
	¼ cup granulated sugar
2 tablespoons all-purpose flour	½ teaspoon cinnamon
	1 pinch salt
2 tablespoons butter, melted	6 tablespoons butter, cut into ½-inch pieces
1 pinch cinnamon	
1 egg, lightly beaten	

1. Preheat the oven to 400°. Toss the fruit with the brown sugar, flour, butter, cinnamon, and egg to coat. Spoon the mixture into one big baking dish or individual ramekins.

2. For the topping, combine the flour, brown sugar, granulated sugar, cinnamon, and salt in a medium bowl. Cut the butter into the mixture until the topping is crumbly. Sprinkle over the fruit in the baking dish.

3. Bake until the fruit is bubbly and the topping turns golden brown, about 25 minutes. Serve warm with ice cream or whipped cream.

DREW'S CAKE, A BLUEBERRY COBBLER
Serves 8

Our youngest son, Drew, has mastered this easy cobbler—which he always calls a cake. What happens is that the berries will, in essence, stew at the bottom of the pan while the cobbler batter bakes above. This "cake" is perfect eaten warm with a big scoop of ice cream.

½ cup (1 stick) butter, softened	1 tablespoon baking powder
1 cup sugar	1 teaspoon lemon zest
2 eggs	1 pinch cinnamon
1 cup milk	3 cups blueberries or other berries
1 cup all-purpose flour	

1. Preheat the oven to 375°. Grease the sides and bottom of a small baking dish with 2 tablespoons of the butter and dust with 3 tablespoons of the sugar. Set aside.

2. In a mixing bowl, whisk together the remaining butter, remaining sugar, and the eggs until light and fluffy. Add the milk and mix well. Whisk in the flour, baking powder, lemon zest, and cinnamon. Pour the berries on the bottom of the prepared baking dish and top with the batter. Bake for 25–30 minutes, until the top is nicely browned. Serve warm.

OUR FAVORITE STRUDEL
Serves 6

In the fall I use apples, pears, and quince in any combination for this filling. The strudel comes together easily when you roll out puff pastry paper thin on a well-floured board. The cake crumbs and dried cherries do a perfect job of absorbing extra moisture from the fruit, keeping the strudel dry and crisp.

1 sheet frozen puff pastry, defrosted	½ cup dried cherries
4 quince, apples, and/or pears, peeled, cored, and roughly chopped	1 teaspoon light brown sugar
1 cup plus 2 pinches granulated sugar	1 teaspoon cinnamon
½ cup (1 stick) butter, diced small	1 pinch salt
½ cup cake crumbs or day-old white bread crumbs	2 eggs, beaten
	¼ cup milk

1. Preheat the oven to 325°. On a well-floured surface, roll out the pastry as thin as possible, creating a large oblong. Combine the fruit, the 1 cup sugar, butter, crumbs, cherries, brown sugar, cinnamon, and salt together in a large mixing bowl and stir gently.

2. With the dough lengthwise before you on the counter, place the filling on the one-third of dough nearest to you. Roll up the dough, away from you (like a burrito), to totally encase the filling in several layers of dough. Make sure the seam ends up on the bottom.

3. With a long spatula, transfer the strudel to a baking sheet. Use a sharp knife to score the strudel at 45° angles 4 times across the top. Bake for 30 minutes.

4. While the strudel is baking, mix together the eggs, milk, and remaining 2 pinches sugar in a small bowl. After 30 minutes, remove the pastry from the oven and use a pastry brush to generously apply the egg mixture to the top and sides. Return the strudel to the oven and bake 30 more minutes, or until the pastry turns a deep golden brown.

BROWN BUTTER–MOLASSES CUPCAKES
Makes 24

These stuffed cupcakes are by far the best-selling dessert at our American Sector restaurant in the National World War II Museum in New Orleans. They're filled with brown butter caramel and frosted with brown butter icing. The caramel filling, a delicious sweet and salty surprise, can also be used as a drizzle over the top of the cupcakes or as a sauce on the side, if you wish.

FOR THE CUPCAKES
- 1⅓ cups all-purpose flour
- 2 teaspoons baking powder
- ½ teaspoon salt
- 3 eggs
- 4 egg yolks
- 1½ cups (3 sticks) butter
- 1¾ cups sugar
- ¾ cup milk
- 1 tablespoon vanilla extract

FOR THE CARAMEL
- ½ cup (1 stick) butter
- 1 cup sugar
- 1 cup heavy cream
- ½ cup molasses
- ½ teaspoon vanilla extract
- 1 teaspoon salt

FOR THE ICING
- ⅓ cup (⅔ stick) butter
- 3 cups powdered sugar
- 2 teaspoons milk
- 1½ teaspoons vanilla extract

1. For the cupcakes, preheat the oven to 325°. Sift together the flour, baking powder, and salt into a mixing bowl and set aside. In a small bowl, whisk together the whole eggs and yolks and set aside.

2. In a large mixing bowl, cream the butter with a handheld mixer until fluffy, then add the sugar all at once and continue creaming until light and fluffy. Add the beaten eggs a little at a time, incorporating well after each addition. Once the eggs are well blended, add the milk and vanilla, mixing well. Fold in the flour mixture by hand, using a rubber spatula. Don't worry if the batter has a few lumps.

3. Fit 24 muffin-tin cups with paper liners and spray with non-stick oil. Pour the batter evenly into each cup. Bake for 30 minutes, or until a knife inserted into the middle of a cupcake comes out clean. Let cool.

4. For the caramel, melt the butter in a saucepan over medium heat, then allow to brown into a nice hazelnut color. Add the sugar, cream, molasses, vanilla, and salt and boil, stirring constantly, for about 5 minutes. Remove from the heat.

5. For the icing, heat the butter in a saucepan over medium heat until brown; remove from the heat. Add the powdered sugar, milk, and vanilla and whisk until smooth.

6. To assemble the cupcakes, cut a quarter-size hole into the top of each cupcake and fill with the brown butter caramel. Spread the brown butter icing over the tops.

YOGURT FRUIT POPS
Makes 6

These pops are both healthy and delicious. My boys will happily eat whatever fruit is in season but they especially love the pops made with strawberries, blueberries, blackberries, and citrus.

- 1½ cups fresh fruit
- 1 cup plain yogurt
- 2½ tablespoons honey (more or less depending on the ripeness of the fruits)

Popsicle molds and sticks

1. Combine half the fruit, the yogurt, and honey in a blender and process until smooth. Cut the remaining fruit into the jar. Divide the mixture among the prepared popsicle molds, making sure to distribute the cut fruit well. Insert wooden popsicle sticks and freeze for 4 hours.

CUPCAKE CENTRAL:
Black Forest Cupcakes
all dressed up and ready
to go, displayed above
caramel-filled Brown
Butter–Molasses
Cupcakes with their
swirly icing. Individual
Warm Any Fruit
Crumbles, on the table.

BLACK FOREST CUPCAKES

Makes 12

Nothing reminds me more of my first day as an intern at the Romantik Hotel Spielweg in Germany than Black Forest Cake and steaming hot coffee. Our version has it all: a rich chocolate cupcake filled with cherries in syrup and topped with whipped cream, chocolate shavings, and a fresh cherry.

1	15-ounce can pitted sweet cherries in syrup
4	ounces dark chocolate, coarsely chopped
1⅓	cups plus 1 tablespoon sugar
¾	cup (1½ sticks) butter
¼	cup plus 1 tablespoon cherry brandy or Kirschwasser
1	egg

1	cup all-purpose flour
2	tablespoons cocoa powder
1	tablespoon baking powder
1	cup heavy cream, whipped
	Dark chocolate, shaved into curls with a vegetable peeler
	Fresh cherries for topping

1. Preheat the oven to 350°. Drain the cherries, reserving the cherries and syrup separately. Combine the cherry syrup, chopped chocolate, sugar, butter, and the ¼ cup brandy in a saucepan. Over low heat, stir until the chocolate has melted. Pour into a large mixing bowl and whisk in the egg. Sift together the flour, cocoa, and baking powder into a small bowl, then fold gently into the chocolate mixture.

2. Fit 12 cups of a muffin tin with paper liners and spray with non-stick oil. Pour the batter evenly into each cup. Bake for 30 minutes, or until the cupcakes are firm to the touch. Let cool for a few minutes and then transfer to a wire rack to cool completely.

3. Mix the remaining 1 tablespoon brandy with the remaining 1 tablespoon sugar and stir into the whipped cream. Cut a quarter-sized hole into the top of each cupcake and fill with canned cherries. Frost with the whipped cream and top with shaved chocolate, and a fresh cherry.

CHESS PIE

Serves 6

One of the nicest gifts I have ever received was a warm chess pie from a friend in rural Alabama. It's a Southern classic that seems almost too simple to be so delicious. By all means make your own pie dough if you can, but I want you to experience this pie, so it's fine to just go ahead and use an unbaked store-bought pie shell if you like. Chess pies were traditionally made with evaporated milk, but you can use the same amount of whole milk.

4	eggs
2	cups sugar
½	cup evaporated milk or whole milk
4	tablespoons butter

2	tablespoons cornmeal
	Zest and juice of 1 lemon
1	unbaked pie shell

1. Preheat the oven to 425°. Combine the eggs, sugar, milk, butter, cornmeal, and lemon zest and juice in a large bowl. Mix until the sugar is dissolved, but do not beat. Pour the filling into the unbaked pie shell.

2. Bake for 10 minutes. Reduce the temperature to 300° and bake until the filling is set, about 40 minutes. Remove from the oven and cool. Serve at room temperature.

BANANAS FLAMBÉ
Serves 6

This is one of my favorite New Orleans classics, and just may be the first dessert I ever made in my life. Down here, we're used to the stagy restaurant presentation, made famous by flamboyant maître d's who sauté the bananas tableside then ignite the pan to the delight of their customers. If setting the alcohol on fire makes you uneasy, don't bother, it's all for show! The truth is the alcohol burns off as it simmers, leaving a richly perfumed caramel banana sauce.

½ cup (1 stick) butter

4 heaping tablespoons brown sugar

6 bananas, peeled and quartered

1 teaspoon orange zest
Juice of 1 orange

1 teaspoon cinnamon

1 dash nutmeg

¼ cup dark rum

3 tablespoons banana liqueur

1 pint vanilla ice cream

1. Heat the butter and brown sugar in a large skillet over high heat, stirring until they have melted into a caramel. Cook for an additional 3 minutes, stirring constantly. Add the bananas, orange zest, orange juice, cinnamon, and nutmeg. Cook for 3 more minutes, stirring gently to coat the bananas.

2. Remove the pan from the heat and, holding the skillet away from you, carefully add the rum and liqueur. Return the skillet to the heat and cook for another 3 minutes. Be aware that the alcohol may ignite if you're cooking over an open flame. Or for deliberate pyrotechnics, you can use a lighter to burn off the alcohol. Serve in individual glasses and top with the vanilla ice cream.

HUMMINGBIRD CAKE

Serves 12

This is a traditional Southern favorite that I especially love when baked by our priest/baker extraordinaire, Father Randy Roux. He challenged Kelly Fields, our pastry chef at Restaurant August, to create a recipe for home cooks that was just as good as his. She rose to the occasion!

FOR THE CAKE

- 3 eggs
- 2 cups sugar
- 1 cup vegetable oil
- 3 cups all-purpose flour
- 1 tablespoon baking powder
- 2 teaspoons cinnamon
- 1½ teaspoons salt
- 2½ cups chopped bananas
- 1½ cups chopped pecans
- 1 8-ounce can crushed pineapple, with juice
- 1 teaspoon vanilla extract

FOR THE ICING

- 1 pound (4 sticks) butter, softened
- 8 ounces cream cheese, room temperature
- 1 cup powdered sugar
- 1 teaspoon vanilla extract
- 2 cups chopped pecans

1. For the cake, preheat the oven to 350°. Butter and flour two 9-inch round cake pans. Set aside.

2. Whisk together the eggs, sugar, and oil in a large mixing bowl. Sift together the flour, baking powder, cinnamon, and salt into a separate bowl, then gently fold into the egg mixture. Stir in the bananas, pecans, pineapple (with its juice), and vanilla.

3. Divide the batter evenly between the prepared cake pans. Bake for 30 minutes, or until a knife inserted into the middles of the cakes comes out clean. Cool cakes in pans until cool enough to transfer to cooling racks.

4. For the icing, cream together the butter and cream cheese with a handheld mixer until well combined. Add the powdered sugar and vanilla and stir until completely incorporated and smooth.

5. Once the cakes have cooled, transfer one cake to a large plate. Cover the top with icing, then place the second layer on top. With a long spatula, spread the icing over the top and side of the cake. Press the larger pecans onto the sides of the cake and fill in with chopped pieces.

LEMON ICE BOX PIE

Serves 8

This old-fashioned dessert is perfect when Meyer lemons are in season, but it's fine to use regular lemons instead. This is a pie you can make in advance and freeze until you're ready to serve it.

- 1 cup graham cracker crumbs
- ⅓ cup (⅔ stick) butter, softened
- 3 eggs, separated
- 14 ounces sweetened condensed milk
- 2 teaspoons lemon zest
- ½ cup fresh Meyer lemon juice or regular lemon juice
- ¼ teaspoon salt
- ½ cup freshly whipped cream

1. Mix together the graham cracker crumbs and butter. Butter the sides and bottom of a 9-inch pie pan, and press the graham cracker mixture into sides and bottom of the pan.

2. In a mixing bowl, whisk together the 3 egg yolks, the condensed milk, lemon zest, lemon juice, and salt. Mix until smooth. In another bowl, beat the 3 egg whites with a handheld mixer until stiff. Gently fold the beaten whites into the lemon mixture. Pour into the prepared pie shell. Wrap well and freeze for at least 3 hours.

3. To serve, remove the pie from freezer, spread the whipped cream over the top, and let sit for 10 minutes before serving.

Acknowledgments

IT IS WITH THE UTMOST HUMILITY that I thank my gracious wife and best friend, Jenifer, for our beautiful life on the bayou with our boys: Brendan, Jack, Luke, and Andrew, who fill each day with utter joy. Countless meals have been inspired by the love that emanates from our home. A meal is so much more than dinner; it can be and should be an act of love. I thank my family for both the grounding and inspiration that they give me and for the patience they showed as I have evolved as a man, a father, and a chef. If asked what my last meal would be, I'd reply, "any Sunday supper at home, cooked with love, for people I love."

I am most grateful to my mother and father for giving me such great memories of food and family and for showing me the importance of our own family table. I learned more there than any classroom could ever teach.

This book would not have been written had I not been pressed by my loving friend and editor Dorothy Kalins, who shares a passion for cooking at home with family and friends. Had it not been for her vision, I would have no way to fully articulate what is most important to me. Dorothy brought together our like-minded creative team: photographer Maura McEvoy (and her daughter Oona); design editor Carol Helms; and the book's designer, the talented Don Morris (who designed *My New Orleans*, too)—all of whom worked on this book with passion and a sense of joy.

My sisters-in-law Mary Beth Berrigan and Kim Bourgault worked tirelessly on organizing pages and pages of longhand chicken scratch, all the while tending to the whims of an impassioned chef and brother who's a bit on the demanding side. Thank you for your love and devotion to our family and to this great book.

I would be remiss if I didn't thank my partner Octavio Mantilla for his support and dedication to my countless causes, none of which would have come to fruition if not for his efforts.

While my dear friends and in-laws Patrick and Erin Berrigan were on vacation, they let us commandeer their beautiful home as a location that captures the essence of our family table. Thank you for your love and support for this project as well as for all my other harebrained ideas.

I really appreciate the passionate efforts of chefs Mike Gulotta, Erick Loos, and Junior Ganucheau, who have supported this project from start to finish. They are not only great chefs but in a sense the family who made it possible for me to dedicate myself to *My Family Table*.

And once again, gratitude to our exemplary publisher Kirsty Melville, who believes in us and lets us go! And to her team at Andrews McMeel, especially Jean Lucas and Deri Reed.

Resources

BACON AND COUNTRY HAM, unsmoked and hickory-smoked by my friend Allan Benton, have become justly famous countrywide.

Benton's Smoky Mountain Country Hams: 2603 Highway 411 North, Madisonville, TN • 423-442-5003 • bentonscountryhams2.com

CREOLE MUSTARD, SPICE MIXES for crab, shrimp, and crawfish boils (available in both dry and liquid form), and seasonings. Although Zatarain's products are readily available in stores throughout the South, distribution in the rest of the country is spotty, so the website is your best bet.

Zatarain's • 888-264-5460 • zatarains.com

FARM-RAISED GEESE You may have a good local purveyor for your holiday goose, but here's an excellent online source. Heritage Foods USA represents farmers who raise animals humanely, which means natural feed, plenty of room to roam, and no antibiotics. They pretty much saved the Bourbon Red Turkey for our Thanksgiving table, plus pork, beef, lamb and more.

Heritage Foods USA: Box 198 402 Graham Ave., Brooklyn, NY • 718-389-0985 • heritagefoodsusa.com

GRITS, CORNMEAL, POLENTA, and other organic, stone-ground products from white, yellow, and blue corn, made fresh by Frank McEwen in his stone burr grist mill to ensure that all the goodness, flavor, and nutrients are retained. He's happy to send you some.

McEwen & Sons: 30620 Highway 25, Wilsonville, AL • 205-669-6605 • fax 205-669-0113 • mcewenandsons.com

PIMENTÓN AND PIQUILLO PEPPERS The Spanish ingredients I love, like smoked paprika—Pimentón de la Vera, available in sweet, bittersweet, and hot—and jars of those wood-fire roasted Piquillo peppers from Lodosa, can be ordered online.

La Tienda • 800-710-4304 • tienda.com

The Spanish Table: stores in Berkeley, Mill Valley, Seattle, Santa Fe • 505-986-0243 • spanishtable.com

SAUSAGES AND BEANS The smoky flavor of pork and chicken sausages makes all the differences in a stew or on the grill.

Jacob's World Famous Andouille & Sausage smokes meats over aged pecan wood and the flavor of their products reflect that care. Also fresh black-eyed peas, and red, white, and lima beans. 505 West Airline Highway, LaPlace, LA • 877-215-7589 • cajunsausage.com

Bailey's Andouille has smoked sausage (hot and mild), andouille, and chicken andouille. 513 West Airline Highway • LaPlace, LA • 985-652-9090 • baileysandouille.com

SHRIMP, CRAB, AND FISH, all from Louisiana waters, are available for shipping from our favorite fishmongers.

Kenney Seafood: My old friend Brian Cappy runs the best seafood shop and will ship what's in season. 400 Pontchartrain Drive, Slidell, LA • 985-643-2717

Louisiana Seafood has excellent information and a helpful Seafood Finder that will connect you with reputable purveyors. louisianaseafood.com

TABASCO PEPPER JELLIES, SAUCES, and an eye-popping array of Tabasco branded products are available online. Pepper jellies are available in Mild or Spicy, and Tabasco sauces are made in a range of potency, from the classic original to Sweet & Spicy, Chipotle, Habenero, and even a Garlic Sauce. Tabasco sauces are available in most supermarkets, but the pepper jellies are not as easily found.

McIlhenny Company: Avery Island, LA • 800-634-9599 • countrystore.tabasco.com

TRUFFLES We've been on a hunt for a domestic truffle and one I can recommend is the fresh black American Perigord grown by Dr. Tom Michaels in the foothills of the Blue Ridge Mountains of eastern Tennessee. Available December through early March.

Tennessee Truffles • 423-747-2939 • tennesseetruffle.com. Dr. Michaels invites direct email queries: tom@tennesseetruffle.com

FARMERS MARKETS Muralist Robert Dafford of Dafford Murals, Lafayette, LA, painted the two walls that anchor the Crescent City Farmers Market, above, at Magazine and Girod Streets in the warehouse district in downtown New Orleans. The market operates there every Saturday morning, then travels to Tulane Square near Audubon Park on Tuesdays and to the corner of Orleans Street and Bayou St. John on Thursdays.

Crescent City Farmers Market • 504-861-4488 • crescentcityfarmersmarket.org

CHEESE, CHARCUTERIE, AND SPECIALTY FOODS Every big city has one, now New Orleans does too—a superb food shop curated by knowledgeable owners. Danielle and Richard Sutton's St. James Cheese Company has changed our lives. Stop by when you're in town.

St. James Cheese Company: 5004 Prytania St., New Orleans, LA • 504-899-4737 • stjamescheese.com

CULINARY ANTIQUES Exquisite table linen, silver serving pieces, copper cookware, and furniture are collected by proprietor Patrick Dunne and sold in his two shops. Examples of Lucullus pieces can be seen on their rich website. Lucullus was generous in lending us beautiful antique tableware for photography, most notably in Goose for the Holidays.

Lucullus Culinary Antiques, Art & Objects: 610 Chartres St., New Orleans, LA • 504-528-9620 • lucullusantiques.com

Metric Conversions & Equivalents

Volume	Metric
¼ teaspoon	1 milliliter
½ teaspoon	2.5 milliliters
¾ teaspoon	4 milliliters
1 teaspoon	5 milliliters
1¼ teaspoons	6 milliliters
1½ teaspoons	7.5 milliliters
1¾ teaspoons	8.5 milliliters
2 teaspoons	10 milliliters
1 tablespoon (½ fluid ounce)	15 milliliters
2 tablespoons (1 fluid ounce)	30 milliliters
¼ cup	60 milliliters
⅓ cup	80 milliliters
½ cup (4 fluid ounces)	120 milliliters
⅔ cup	160 milliliters
¾ cup	180 milliliters
1 cup (8 fluid ounces)	240 milliliters
1¼ cups	300 milliliters
1½ cups (12 fluid ounces)	360 milliliters
1⅔ cups	400 milliliters
2 cups (1 pint)	460 milliliters
3 cups	700 milliliters
4 cups (1 quart)	0.95 liter
1 quart plus ¼ cup	1 liter
4 quarts (1 gallon)	3.8 liters

Weight	
¼ ounce	7 grams
½ ounce	14 grams
¾ ounce	21 grams
1 ounce	28 grams
1¼ ounces	35 grams
1½ ounces	42.5 grams
1⅔ ounces	45 grams
2 ounces	57 grams
3 ounces	85 grams
4 ounces (¼ pound)	113 grams
5 ounces	142 grams
6 ounces	170 grams
7 ounces	198 grams
8 ounces (½ pound)	227 grams
16 ounces (1 pound)	454 grams
35.25 ounces (2.2 pounds)	1 kilogram

Length	
⅛ inch	3 millimeters
¼ inch	6 millimeters
½ inch	1¼ centimeters
1 inch	2½ centimeters
2 inches	5 centimeters
2 ½ inches	6 centimeters
4 inches	10 centimeters
5 inches	13 centimeters
6 inches	15¼ centimeters
12 inches (1 foot)	30 centimeters

To Convert	Multiply
Ounces to grams	Ounces by 28.35
Pounds to kilograms	Pounds by .454
Teaspoons to milliliters	Teaspoons by 4.93
Tablespoons to milliliters	Tablespoons by 14.79
Fluid ounces to milliliters	Fluid ounces by 29.57
Cups to milliliters	Cups by 236.59
Cups to liters	Cups by .236
Pints to liters	Pints by .473
Quarts to liters	Quarts by .946
Gallons to liters	Gallons by 3.785
Inches to centimeters	Inches by 2.54

OVEN TEMPERATURES

To convert Fahrenheit to Celsius, subtract 32 from Fahrenheit, multiply the result by 5, then divide by 9.

Description	Fahrenheit	Celsius	British Gas Mark
Very cool	200°	95°	0
Very cool	225°	110°	¼
Very cool	250°	120°	½
Cool	275°	135°	1
Cool	300°	150°	2
Warm	325°	165°	3
Moderate	350°	175°	4
Moderately hot	375°	190°	5
Fairly hot	400°	200°	6
Hot	425°	220°	7
Very hot	450°	230°	8
Very hot	475°	245°	9

COMMON INGREDIENTS & THEIR APPROXIMATE EQUIVALENTS

1 cup uncooked white rice = 185 grams

1 cup all-purpose flour = 140 grams

1 stick butter (4 ounces • ½ cup • 8 tablespoons) = 110 grams

1 cup butter (8 ounces • 2 sticks • 16 tablespoons) = 220 grams

1 cup brown sugar, firmly packed = 225 grams

1 cup granulated sugar = 200 grams

Information compiled from a variety of sources, including *Recipes into Type* by Joan Whitman and Dolores Simon (Newton, MA: Biscuit Books, 2000); *The New Food Lover's Companion* by Sharon Tyler Herbst (Hauppauge, NY: Barron's, 1995); and *Rosemary Brown's Big Kitchen Instruction Book* (Kansas City, MO: Andrews McMeel, 1998).

Index

Quick Pickled Vegetables, 24–25
Ramen noodles, 88
Ratatouille, 48
resources, 254–55
rice
 arborio, 9
 Blue Crab & Sausage Stew, 196
 brown jasmine, 9
 Crown Roast of Pork with Dirty Rice Dressing, 202–3
 Curried Anything, 21
 noodles, 11, 90
 Pork & Sausage Jambalaya, 70
 Rice Pudding, 240
 Risotto of Almost Anything, 13
 Stuffed Bell Peppers, 70–71
 wine vinegar, 11, 52, 85–86, 88–89, 121, 146, 161, 166, 172, 175–76, 187–88, 195, 200, 215
Risotto of Almost Anything, 13
roasted dishes, 36
 Basic Pan Sauce for All Roast Meats, 38
 Crispy Roast Ducklings, 44
 Crown Roast of Pork with Dirty Rice Dressing, 202–3
 Herb-Roasted Chicken, 40–41
 Olive Oil-Roasted Cauliflower, 48
 Pan-Roasted Grouper with Shellfish Tomato Sauce, 129
 Pasta with Roast Chicken & Tomatoes, 28
 Perfect Roast Leg of Lamb, 44
 Pork Rib Roast, 45
 Roast Beet Salad, 52–53
 Roast Goose, 211, 218–19
 Roasted Pear Salad, 194–95
 Roasted Red Pepper Salad, 166
 Rosemary & Garlic Roast Fingerling Potatoes, 50
 Slow-Cooked Beef Chuck Roast, 46–47
 Slow-Roasted Pork Shoulder, 38–39
 Whole Roasted Sole with Brown Butter, 124–25
Rosemary & Garlic Roast Fingerling Potatoes, 50

S

saffron, 27
salads
 Asian Chicken Salad, 88
 Black-Eyed Pea Salad, 176–77
 Coleslaw, 175
 Fried Eggplant Salad, 146
 Fruit Salad with Champagne & Mint, 192–93
 Grilled Avocado & Tomato Salad, 173
 My Favorite Potato Salad, 174–75
 Roast Beet Salad, 52–53
 Roasted Pear Salad, 194–95
 Roasted Red Pepper Salad, 166
 Sugar Snap Pea Salad with Pecans, 198–99
salmon, 120–21
Salt-Baked Striped Bass, 130–31
sambal chili paste, 11, 127
Sambal Mayonnaise, 127
satsuma oranges, 122–23, 184
 Louisiana Satsuma Cocktail, 192
 Poached Eggs & Satsuma Hollandaise Over Crab Cakes, 190–91
 Satsuma Hollandaise, 190–91
sauces, 85
 Basic Pan Sauce for All Roast Meats, 38
 Cherry Tomato Five-Minute Sauce, 10, 26, 70–71
 for fish, 118
 green, 164
 hoisin, 11, 86, 89
 Light Tomato Sauce, 133
 marinade, 164, 200
 pan drippings, 40
 Pepper Jelly Barbecue Sauce, 172
 poaching, 119
 resources, 255
 Satsuma Hollandaise Sauce, 190–91
 Shellfish Tomato Sauce, 129
sausages
 Baked Beans, 161
 Blue Crab & Sausage Stew, 196
 Crown Roast of Pork with Dirty Rice Dressing, 202–3
 grilling, 165
 Our Italian Wedding Soup, 93
 Pork & Sausage Jambalaya, 70
 resources, 254
 school night, 77–82
 Asian Chicken Salad, 88
 Beef Noodle Bowls, 86–87
 Cauliflower Mac & Cheese, 83
 Chicken & Noodle Pan-Fry, 89
 Creamy Heirloom Tomato Soup with
 Grilled Ham & Cheese, 94–95
 Easy Pork Grillades, 94
 Hearty Baked Pasta, 90–91
 Heat & Serve Chili, 84
 Our Italian Wedding Soup, 93
 Sloppy Joe Sliders, 85
 Southern Soup au Pistou, 55, 92–93
 Vietnamese Noodle Soup, 90–91
scrambled eggs, 102
seafood seasoning, 25, 26, 108
Seafood-Stuffed Cabbage, 74–75
searing, 36
Seaton, Kerry, 139
Seaton, Willie Mae, 139, 145
Seaton, Slim Charles, 145
Sedacek, Lou, 104
shallots, 38, 74, 164, 191, 195, 218
 Crispy Roast Ducklings, 44
Shaya, Alon, 167
Shellfish Broth, 26
Shellfish Tomato Sauce, 129
shrimp, 116
 for barbecue, 156
 Eggplant Dressing, 55
 Pickled Shrimp, 186–87
 Risotto of Almost Anything, 13
 Seafood-Stuffed Cabbage, 74–75
 Shellfish Broth, 26
 Stuffed Mushrooms, 196
Simple Cheese Omelette, 103
Simple Meat Ragout for Any Pasta, 17
Sloppy Joe Sliders, 85
Slow-Cooked Beef Chuck Roast, 46–47
Slow-Cooked Venison, 73
Slow-Roasted Pork Shoulder, 38–39
Smitty's Market (Lockhart, Texas), 157
smoked paprika (pimentón), 7–8, 10, 70
smokers, 157–58, 160
smoothies, 192
snapper, 133
Snickerdoodles, 234, 237
sole, 124–25
soups
 Creamy Any Vegetable Soup, 14
 Creamy Heirloom Tomato Soup with Grilled Ham & Cheese, 94–95
 Creamy Lentil Soup, 216–17
 Our Italian Wedding Soup, 93
 Southern Soup au Pistou, 55, 92–93
 Vietnamese Noodle Soup, 90–91
 Yellow Tomato Gazpacho, 187